family living

family living

creating the
perfect family home

Judith Wilson

photography by Debi Treloar

RYLAND
PETERS
& SMALL
LONDON NEW YORK

Designer Fiona Walker
Commissioning editor Annabel Morgan
Location research Judith Wilson and
Claire Hector
Production Patricia Harrington
Art director Gabriella Le Grazie
Publishing director Alison Starling

Stylist Judith Wilson

First published in the United Kingdom in 2003
by Ryland Peters & Small
20–21 Jockey's Fields
London WC1R 4BW
www.rylandpeters.com

10 9 8 7 6 5 4 3

Text © Judith Wilson 2003

Design and photographs © Ryland Peters
& Small 2003

Printed and bound in China.

ISBN-10: 1-84172-405-X
ISBN-13: 978-1-84172-405-8.

A CIP record for this book is available from
the British Library.

contents

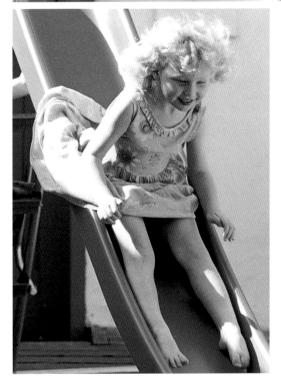

Nothing beats family living. Chaotic and noisy it may be, but it's also sociable, fun, relaxing and hilarious. For parents and kids alike, there's incalculable merit to a home where everyone can gather *en famille* or invite friends over for an impromptu supper. Lots of space, though always a bonus, is not the issue. Creating the perfect family home is about maximizing the potential of the space you already have.

The presence of kids demands long-term planning. Children canter through developmental phases, and swiftly graduate from needing kitchen-floor space to a bedroom hideaway. The key is flexibility, allowing room functions to be switched with minimal hassle. Plan for that, and the need for serial moving is reduced. It makes financial sense to create a home to grow into, and kids will appreciate the continuity.

introduction

Spatially speaking, this book is matched to the ebb and flow of real family life. Part One is about creating free-flowing activity zones. Part Two accepts that parents and kids both need time out, so concerns peaceful zones. And, as every parent knows, a family home only works like clockwork if it's well-organized and practical, so Part Three sorts surfaces, storage and spaces in between.

No family home should be a show home – it's children's clutter that creates its true soul – but it shouldn't be a mess either. Enjoy creating a welcoming, beautiful, even sophisticated, living space and your kids will respect it and enjoy sharing it with you. And never underestimate the emotional power of the childhood home. Make it a fun place to be now, and your children will keep on returning long after they've flown the nest.

**multifunctional kitchens
communal sitting rooms
playrooms and media rooms**

activity zones

'Our kitchen is a very sociable space and the core of the home where everyone meets.'

JEMIMA, AGE 17

'What matters is that we are all together as one unit, even if I'm cooking, my son is watching TV and the baby is on the floor.'

KATE, MOTHER

'We like the idea of a space role-reversal: an indoor space where kids can do outdoor things – rope-climbing, cycling – and an outdoors where we can eat and entertain.'

HIRO, FATHER

multifunctional kitchens

Modern-day family life revolves around the kitchen. Hungry kids always make a beeline for it, and it's the focal point for family meals. The best-planned kitchens also provide a welcoming environment where children will want to study, watch television and chat with their friends or (you never know) their parents. So create an open-plan, bright yet functional space where everyone, including little ones, can enjoy sociable family living.

BELOW: Even in a small kitchen, try to provide several seating choices, from a formal dining table to a breakfast bar. On a daily basis, kids have more room to spread out with homework on one tabletop, while supper is laid on another. There's also double the chair space for larger family gatherings. For a cohesive look, pick matching chair and stool styles.

RIGHT: When designing an island unit that doubles as a breakfast bar, ensure there's sufficient leg room for adults as well as kids beneath the worktop, and that stools will tuck underneath, so small children zooming around won't crash into them.

LEFT: An island unit is the most sociable and useful component in a family kitchen. Perfect as a food preparation area or breakfast bar, or for dishing up food, islands work best when positioned centrally, dividing eating and cooking areas. Yet they can easily become a dumping ground for school books or last night's tea tray, so be strict about keeping the top clear.
BELOW: During a typical weekend, families can get through an alarming number of glasses and crockery, so make life easy by amassing a generous selection. Open shelves, positioned close to the dishwasher, make all that unloading and table-laying much easier.

The whole point about creating a multifunctional space is that it provides room for cooking, eating and sitting areas – all together. The advantages are obvious. Not only is there more room for kids to gather, so they are less likely to disappear upstairs, but if everyone wants to do something different (as is common in larger families), varying needs can be accommodated. Little ones can scoot around on bikes, adults can cook and homework can get underway.

Given that the kitchen is the nerve-centre of the family home, it should be in an accessible location. Close to the front door makes for quick school exits, toast in hand, while a rear kitchen with garden access is great for smaller children. In loft spaces or one-level apartments, a centrally situated open-plan kitchen is more sociable than a conventional galley at the end of a corridor. And in a detached property, make the kitchen the heart of the home, by placing it right by the back door. If the kitchen is easy to get to, kids will be more likely to linger, long after their hunger pangs are satisfied.

THIS PAGE: When kids are little and play regularly in the kitchen, plan enough units to accommodate their needs as well as storing cooking equipment. Low-level storage makes it easy for them to reach everything from art materials to videos. Plenty of drawers, with easy-to-grab handles, are often more helpful for organizing than deep cupboards.

OPPOSITE: In an open-plan multifunctional kitchen, use a choice of surfaces to delineate different activity areas. Here, wood veneer sections off the dining area, while painted doors indicate storage and a ground-floor toilet.

THIS PAGE AND OPPOSITE, ABOVE: Bespoke carpentry means even a narrow room can accommodate a dining table, seating bench and food preparation zones. Essential appliances can be fitted into an island unit, and wall cupboards extended up to the ceiling. OPPOSITE, BELOW: Kids and adults alike will appreciate funky touches such as glitter mosaic tiles or a glass worktop with colourful under-worktop lighting.

If you're adapting an existing property and the kitchen is inconveniently sited, then consider relocating it. What may seem an extravagant option can be a sound investment if it makes the difference between staying put or moving house as your family's needs change or expand. Try to use an architect (if funds are limited, many will work on a consultancy-only basis, providing ideas and drawings) but choose one familiar with family life, so the emphasis is on great space, not just designer statements.

If the kitchen is too small to incorporate additional living space, then knocking through into an adjacent room or hallway can be one solution. If it's not an option to move existing kitchen units, removing the upper part of the wall between the kitchen and living area will create a sociable connection. Even installing double doors to link the kitchen with the dining or sitting room will make a vast difference.

When searching for a family home, make a big kitchen a top priority. Trendy city-dwellers are exploring not only lofts, but also commercial buildings such as garages and workshops, which offer extensive living space. New-build family homes are a brilliant option, providing the chance to truly redefine family living spaces. Don't discount the Thirties semi. Its large kitchen, sitting and dining rooms can be knocked into open-plan living quarters, and many have the added advantage of a big suburban garden.

When planning a kitchen, think in terms of free-flowing zones, rather than having conventional kitchen units at one end of the room and a dining table at the other. Blurring the boundaries maximizes the available space. For example, a kitchen island unit could double as a breakfast bar, which obviates the need for a separate table (and is perfect for snacking kids). And placing all cupboards or units along one wall, rather than in the traditional L- or U-shape, means more floor space is freed up for little ones to run around. A single bank of wall cupboards designed to hold not just kitchen equipment and tableware but toys and books too will save on space and provide a more cohesive look to the room.

The best family kitchens boast efficient, capacious appliances. A dishwasher is essential, but think not just in terms of a large one (multiple guests for Sunday lunch) but also a quiet model that won't

ABOVE: In a new-build home or modern extension, a kitchen will become truly multifunctional if designed to lead directly onto outdoor space, linked with floor-to-ceiling sliding glass doors. While small kids benefit from extra play space, grown-ups or teenagers can entertain inside or out.

OPPOSITE: A cutting-edge contemporary kitchen can still be family-friendly, when materials are carefully chosen. With its wipe-clean leather chairs, durable limestone floor and hardwearing catering-style stainless-steel worktops, this kitchen is practical by day, and sleek and sophisticated at night.

disturb post-supper television viewing. A built-in double oven, freestanding industrial-style range or an Aga will cater for large numbers, but team this with a microwave – essential for late-night teenage snacks. A six- rather than four-burner hob is very helpful. Also consider an American-style fridge, combined with a freezer (stored in a garage or cellar) for large-capacity food supplies.

Plan the cooking zone layout with you and the kids in mind, so it's easy for them to help with food preparation. Little ones love to bake with adults, while older children enjoy the independence of creating packed lunches and simple meals. Consider a kitchen with under-counter cupboards only, so children can reach utensils with ease. Freestanding kitchen workstations and island units, accessible from all sides, are also child-friendly. A fridge at floor-level and a worktop microwave are safer than those built in at adult eye-level.

In a space where cooking and relaxing zones merge, plan for the inevitable messy, post-cooking kitchen. An island unit with a higher wall on the sitting side can bisect work and play areas, neatly

concealing kitchen clutter. In a loft space, a centrally sited kitchen zone can be screened off with wall-to-floor sliding MDF or sandblasted glass doors. If you are creating a new open-plan space, retain a slim section of wall to divide cooking and relaxing areas. Fit one side with kitchen storage cupboards, and the other with an inset TV and a giant pinboard. And install a good extractor fan, so cooking smells don't stray to the rest of the house.

In decorative terms, the family kitchen should tread a fine line between looking cosy (for small children), stylish (for grown-up dinner parties) and a little bit funky (for teenagers). It must also be supremely practical. That's not impossible to achieve. What matters most (as a good kitchen should last a decade plus), is that the essential bones – flooring, cupboard fronts, worktops – are classic and plain. Furniture and accessories can be matched to your kids' ages, tastes and needs as these evolve. For example, a plain white kitchen might be accessorized first with pink mini chairs and table, swiftly followed by sociable wooden benches and gold glitter splashback tiles.

OPPOSITE, BELOW LEFT: Family life is busy enough without endlessly cleaning the kitchen, so pick easy-care surfaces. Stainless steel, glass or stone splashbacks can all be wiped clean. Alternatively, use tiles, from bright mosaics to hand-thrown ceramics, to inject strong colour.

OPPOSITE, BELOW RIGHT: Casual, robust furniture is the sensible option. Antique wood refectory or marble-topped bakery styles, or a zinc-topped junk-shop find make unusual yet relaxed choices, especially when teamed with mismatched wood or metal café chairs.

RIGHT AND BELOW: When faced with a very large open-plan multifunctional kitchen, such as in a loft, it can be tempting to 'fill' the space by dividing it into eating, cooking and sitting zones. More usefully, plan to retain a generous amount of open floor space (perfect for parties, as well as small kids running around), then group the activity zones close together for intimacy and practicality. Grown-ups don't want to carry hot dishes far from cooker to dining table, and kids like perching on a chair close enough to chat to parents preparing food.

LEFT: Efficiency is all-important in the kitchen, so even if the room is small, it makes sense to incorporate generously sized appliances and compromise on storage. Pans and plates can be stacked on open shelves, but a full-size dishwasher is an absolute essential.

BELOW AND OPPOSITE: In a corridor-style kitchen, even the smallest table makes the room user-friendly for kids too. If there's no space for a freestanding piece, consider a built-in tabletop squeezed into an alcove with stools neatly tucked beneath.

Do use colour in the kitchen. Children respond instinctively to it, and will find a kitchen with a tangerine-painted wall or leaf-green rubber floor much more fun to spend time in. Colour also lends instant atmosphere. If you're a white-and-stainless-steel fan, think instead of using colourful accessories. Cheerful shades may also help to 'zone' the areas within a very large space.

When kids are around, it pays to choose practical, wipe-clean cupboard fronts. For trendy minimalists, white or coloured laminates, stainless steel, sand-blasted glass and spray-painted MDF are all great cupboard door options. A more classic look, as good with country as with trendy furniture, is achieved with painted tongue-and-groove or panelled wood. Invest in a quality work surface, as it needs to withstand lots of wear and tear. Stainless steel and solid wood look all the better for a few scuffs, while granite and marble provide a sleeker finish. And Corian, while expensive, is incredibly hard-wearing and comes in myriad colours. Less costly options include concrete and laminates.

DAVID WATTS, Dealer in BARLEY MEAL, POLLARD, BRAN &c

The kitchen floor must be robust. This is the heaviest traffic area of the house, and the floor will need to withstand food spills, riotous games and muddy feet. Solid wood flooring may prove more enduring than some wood laminates. Consider reclaimed boards or painted floorboards, which are easy to touch up. Stone and painted concrete are hard-wearing options, but more sensible for small children are lino or rubber, which come in fabulous bright colours. Also check out unusual choices, such as squash-court flooring, which is springy underfoot.

Great storage is vital in a family kitchen. First, there's the basic cooking kit, with multiple pots and pans. Seasoned parents also know that bottle sterilizers and the baby mouli soon give way to extensive bakeware (from muffin trays to birthday-cake tins) and lolly and jelly moulds, not to mention all those appliances, from ice-cream makers to espresso machines. Plenty of deep drawers, rather than cupboards, often make for the easiest access, though locate frequently used appliances on the worktop.

When a kitchen constitutes the main living space, there must also be storage for leisure materials, from board games to paints. The neatest solution is to match cupboards to kitchen units. If the kitchen is unfitted, go for open shelves lined with rows of identical labelled boxes (rattan, cardboard or metal) or a quirky, junk-shop armoire fitted with labelled containers of varying sizes, to help kids (and you) stay organized.

Tableware also needs a home. Even a small family should have double or triple quantities of everything. Locate everything near the dining area, and keep everyday stuff low down so little ones can help set the table. To suit classic kitchens, a distressed wooden dresser is a great storage option; in trendier homes, stash everything in sleek floor-to-ceiling cupboards or a Sixties sideboard. What about good family tableware? A robust set of white tableware is an excellent start. To this, add jolly coloured tumblers, patterned bowls and trendy tablemats. Younger children will also enjoy personalizing the table with numbered napkin rings or named mugs.

Shared mealtimes are crucial to family life, so while a breakfast bar is great for quick meals, ensure there is a table and enough seating for everyone to sit down together. Get as big a dining table as possible, preferably an extending one (a round table is good for smaller spaces). As the table will be used alternately for homework, model-making or daily paperwork, choose one with a hard-wearing surface, so there's no need for a protective cloth. Solid wood, stainless steel or zinc, laminates and painted MDF are all ideal.

The best seating options allow for extra guests at a moment's notice. Children enjoy squashing onto wooden benches or a built-in banquette upholstered in wipe-clean leather or vinyl. Stools are cool for teenagers, from traditional laboratory ones to modern classics in metal. It's a good idea to choose stacking or folding chairs so extras are easily stored – go for plastic, metal or wood, and save upholstery for the empty-nest years!

In a multi-zoned space, plan your lighting carefully. While cooking and play zones should have excellent low-voltage overhead lighting, the dining area needs a decorative pendant

OPPOSITE: Cheerful colour is essential if the kitchen is to be welcoming. As well as painting walls, consider coloured laminate worktops, painted MDF units and bright tiles. Coloured surfaces are less likely to show up scuffs than pristine white.

ABOVE LEFT: The kitchen is the ideal space to show off children's art, be it splashes of paint or a teenage masterpiece.
ABOVE RIGHT AND BELOW: When space is tight, an upholstered banquette can double up as comfy seating for dinner and a television-watching sofa.

light fitting, preferably on a dimmer switch so you can set the right tone for dinner parties or use the light turned right up as task lighting for homework.

If space permits, it's great to have a comfy zone in the kitchen, even if you have a sitting room too. Small two-seater sofas, bean bags or a daybed take up minimal room, and add splashes of jolly colour if sensibly loose-covered in bright cotton plains or a funky retro print. Combine with a low-level television, built into a storage unit, inset in an alcove, or wall-mounted on an extending bracket so it can be viewed from the cooking zone too. And don't forget music. Whether it's nursery rhymes or hip hop, everyone should be able to dance in the kitchen. So a good sound system, with concealed or wall-mounted speakers, is essential, especially for parties. And while sorting technology, don't forget phone points for the telephone and the laptop.

However well-planned, a multifunctional space only works at full capacity if organization is spot-on. Keep track of school activities and artwork by providing a large pinboard or painting a section of wall with magnetic paint. Add a whiteboard so everyone takes responsibility for relaying phone messages and shopping lists. And don't forget a large clock, so being late for school – or breaking the curfew – is never an option!

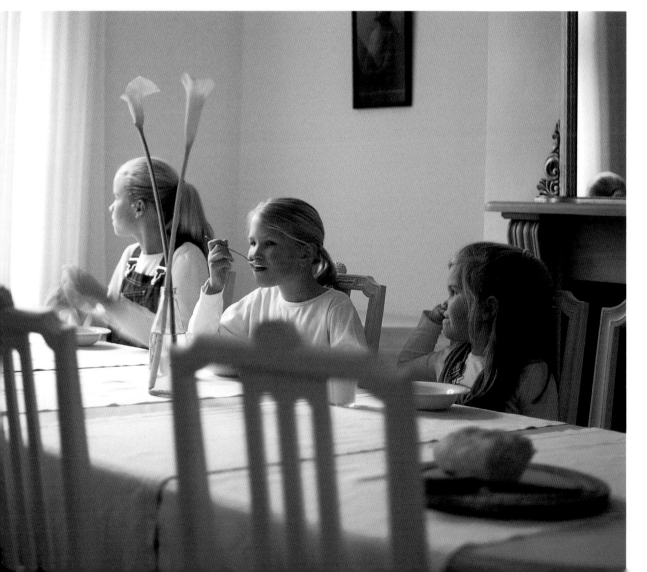

OPPOSITE: The family kitchen is for grown-ups to enjoy as well as children, so keen cooks should choose a casual, unfitted style with all their utensils nearby. Not only will this encourage budding foodies, but there's less pressure to tidy up than in a minimalist-style room. LEFT: Kitchen eating is about casual entertaining, but plan your accessories so the dining table can look formal on high days and holidays. Pick easy-wash tablecloths, from rough antique linens to a denim table runner that won't stain if Ribena (or red wine) gets spilled.

communal sitting rooms

The best family sitting rooms are cosy enough for lazy Sunday afternoons, and chic enough for grown-up entertaining. A flexible furniture layout helps to accommodate larger numbers on high days and holidays. Don't make the sitting room a no-go zone for younger children. Choose practical furnishings that everyone can enjoy without worrying about spills. Textures should be warming and touchy-feely, from fluffy throws to a soft rug underfoot.

BELOW LEFT AND RIGHT: Personalize the sitting room with decorative finds – even little children appreciate pretty things, and jewel-coloured velvet cushions, a twinkling chandelier, or a giant canvas will appeal to kids and adults alike. Place anything breakable out of reach until the later years, and for practicality, choose shabby chic over precious antiques. Counter grown-up choices with easy-care whitewashed floorboards and washable loose covers. OPPOSITE: Don't automatically rule out enjoying serious contemporary art. Children will enjoy the stimulation of colourfully hung walls and find their own 'pictures' within abstract displays.

Even if much of the family's weekday activity is kitchen-based, if space permits it's great to have a separate sitting room. In the evenings, parents of small children will enjoy a toy-free zone, and older kids will also appreciate a quiet spot to escape to. It's helpful for kids to learn the difference between a sophisticated entertaining space and kitchen living – they are easily taught to respect nice things. Make rules early on, then don't nag. You don't want cupcakes on the sofa, but there's nothing wrong with the pop-up tent if it means everyone is together.

Think about your sitting room. Does its location fit the lifestyle and ages of your children? With little ones, it's a boon to have one close to the kitchen, so you can keep track of who's up to what. With teenagers, a first floor drawing room might put a peaceful distance between you and their friends. Do you use the space to your best advantage? Many families have a formal room for 'best', but avoid it like the plague. If this is you, ask yourself why? Is the room dark, is it too big or too cold?

THIS PAGE: It's a fact of family life that most kids sprawl on the floor. Make it cosy with a sheepskin or fluffy deep-pile wool rug, and add character with a contemporary design, choosing from Smarties-spotted styles to abstract squiggles or *faux* animal skins.

OPPOSITE, ABOVE: Furnish each chair with a side table, so there's less likelihood of drinks getting spilled.

OPPOSITE, BELOW LEFT AND RIGHT: In a contemporary sitting room, tailor-made wall-mounted storage can hold everything from videos to family snaps.

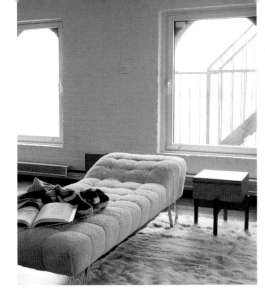

Often the best solution is to swap rooms around. Perhaps a dingy room could be converted into a media room, while a sunny first floor bedroom does service as a sitting room instead?

Consider who will use the sitting room daily, what numbers are likely to swell to on weekends, and what activities will take place there? As well as the inevitable socializing, there will probably be television viewing and family games. Ask your older children how they anticipate using the room. Once you've got the answers, the space can be zoned accordingly. In L-shaped or long narrow sitting rooms, it's useful to bisect the space into a main social area with a reading zone at the other end. A very large room might be divided with double doors, with the stereo in one, the TV in the other, thus controlling dual noise sources.

Decide on the room's natural focus. If it's the television, accept it with good grace and arrange the furniture accordingly. Choose an attractive, contemporary television on a stand, and put it centre stage, instead of trying to conceal it in a cabinet.

OPPOSITE: The best family sitting rooms are full of cosy personal memorabilia. Frame family snaps simply, then make a decorative, ever-changing feature out of them by propping casually on several shelves. Let the kids have the freedom to add and take away as new ones appear.
LEFT AND RIGHT: Even in a busy family home, it's still possible to enjoy the versatility and sophistication of that eternal sitting room classic – the white armchair. Practical options include pre-shrunk washable cotton, calico, linen/cotton mixes or denim, made up into loose covers, or wipe-clean white leather or vinyl.

A fireplace also creates a wonderful focus. A real fire, or gas-effect log one, can do wonders in winter to tempt anti-social teenagers downstairs, and there's nothing quite like gathering round it for making home seem a cosy place to be. When little ones are around, always use a fireguard, and keep matches well out of the way.

Decoratively speaking, start with surfaces. Aim to create a relaxed and cosy visual tone, appealing to grown-ups and kids alike. Good soft colours include dusky pinks and neutrals, from mushroom to biscuit, or warming shades like terracotta. With small kids around, painted walls are easy to touch up, while patterned wallpapers or textured finishes are excellent for concealing little fingerprints. Children naturally gravitate downwards, so will beg for soft flooring. Either choose neutral carpeting – 100 per cent wool, so it cleans easily – or wooden floorboards. Add a rug that can be rolled up for parties. Don't choose sisal, as it's too scratchy to lie on.

Great seating is crucial. There should be a comfortable spot for every member of the family, plus spare for visiting friends. If your children are still little, often the best option is a vast three-seater sofa, so the whole family can cuddle up together. Older (and bigger) kids

LEFT: If there is space, some families prefer the option of a formal sitting room, for grown-up entertaining, combined with a cosy den for TV-watching on week nights. But don't opt for sophisticated finishes at the expense of banning the kids entirely – they should still be able to pile in on high days and holidays. The ideal mix is chic furniture outlines – streamlined oblong sofas, curvy occasional chairs – combined with upholstery in sensible dark shades, so marks won't show.
BELOW AND OPPOSITE: Always include some occasional or modular seating that is easy to move around – from upholstered cubes to a single armchair – so impromptu quiet corners are easily arranged.

might prefer two smaller sofas, placed sociably opposite one another, plus assorted armchairs, or an L-shaped modular seating unit. For teenagers – or weary adults – a daybed is perfect for lounging, as is a large upholstered stool on castors for small kids. The more pieces of furniture you can have on wheels, the better, so that for larger social gatherings, floor space is easily cleared.

Upholstery fabrics must be practical, because all the food rules in the world won't prevent the inevitable spills. But you can still have attractive, beautiful textiles. Good fitted-upholstery options include wool bouclé or wool mixes, chenille or velvet. Pick them in deep, rich shades and they won't show marks: aubergine, charcoal, and berry tones are all trendy, pretty choices. If you're after muted, pale colours, white or pastel upholstery is still an option, but opt for loose covers in a washable fabric such as preshrunk denim. Leather and vinyl, in brown, black or white, are truly sensible choices.

Children love fun, versatile seating. They particularly enjoy low-level options that can be drawn up to a coffee table for afternoon tea or for television watching. Consider beanbags or seating cubes, which can look very sophisticated in leather or felt. Also include at least one chair that affords privacy for reading: a wing chair, rocking chair or a modern-day classic like the Egg swivel chair. Children love the novelty of a frivolous piece of furniture. If your style is traditional, why not upholster one piece in a bright colour – a scarlet armchair, say – or look for a funky retro swivel chair if your room is contemporary.

Where possible, pick occasional furniture with a dual function, to save space and cater for varied demands. A big coffee table is useful for multiple teenage coffee cups as well as providing a base for board games, but pick one with shelf storage beneath for stacks of comics and books. A Sixties-style low sideboard offers great display space on top, and can hold an entire family's photo albums and video collection. It's also nice to have a permanently set-up table, with dining chairs, for a jigsaw in

OPPOSITE: If there's no space for a separate drawing room, it's still possible to engineer a relaxed ambient mood in a communal sitting area, even if it leads directly off the kitchen. Mark the difference between the two areas by choosing the occasional piece of curvaceous furniture, from a deep swivel chair to an antique armoire, a round coffee table to a chandelier. Practicality still matters: these armoires, for example, hold toys and tableware. THIS PAGE: When kids are young, furnish the sitting area sparsely, so there's plenty of central floor space for the sprawling out and endless game playing.

progress or adult card games. Whatever the furniture, go for pieces in robust materials like wood or painted MDF, rather than perspex (which will scratch) or glass (too many sharp corners). Distressed junk-shop antiques, rather than rare and precious ones, are also preferable. If smaller children are around, think about safety. Tiny side tables can go flying, as can standard lamps and floor-standing glass vases.

Every sitting room needs storage. Make a list of what needs to live here, from books and videos to photo albums and board games. For the most serene mood, pick storage with doors that conceal clutter. If the room is contemporary, consider a freestanding cabinet or fitted flush wall units, or if traditional, a bureau teamed with panelled alcove cupboards. Help kids keep things tidy by filling each piece of storage with smaller labelled boxes. Books are essential in the sitting room, providing stimulus

OPPOSITE, ABOVE AND BELOW: In a one-level apartment, or a through drawing room where two rooms have been knocked into one, combining a comfortable sitting area with a dining room is a sociable arrangement. Grown-ups can chat over dinner, while the kids chill out with the TV. It's vital to be able to separate each area, so double doors or sliding screens should be installed. THIS PAGE: Alternatively, you could plan a more formal seating arrangement at one end of the room and a cosy snug at the other, complete with squashy armchairs and wall-to-wall books, videos, magazines and CDs.

for children and creating instant ambience for everyone. Consider fitted shelves in an alcove, a wall of contemporary, thick-fronted shelves or a freestanding bookcase. Whatever the style, position the kids' books on lower shelves for easy access.

When choosing accessories for the sitting room, don't forget this is the kids' space, too. Children will respond to an overly formal, pared-down room by refusing to sit in it – it's that simple. So ask them which precious things they would like to include. Great choices include 'found' objects picked up on a family holiday, from shells to a twisted piece of driftwood, or a child's artwork, beautifully framed. The sitting room is also the place for family snaps. Tuck them into an overmantel mirror or have them framed to fill a whole wall. Kids, as well as visitors, will enjoy a collage of photos of parents, grandparents, babies and kids. You could commission a portrait of your kids – the most personal artwork of all.

The sitting room is for relaxing in, so make it comfortable. Small children are tactile creatures, and love to cocoon themselves in something soft while winding down before bed. Teenagers will do the same. Furnish sofas with fat, feather-filled cushions in touchy-feely textiles like velvet and mohair. Always have a few throws to hand, in something cosy like ribbed wool or chenille, and don't be precious about little ones using them too. Finally, remember that kids – just like grown-ups – appreciate fresh flowers and delicious smells. Light a scented candle spiked with fig or vanilla, and every seat in the room will be occupied in twenty seconds flat.

OPPOSITE AND LEFT: It's impossible to create a formal sitting area in an open-plan space where a kitchen table or play area are also visible. Instead, go for a colourful, relaxed bohemian look. Kids love this laid-back style, because a little mess doesn't matter, and for grown-ups, with the lights down low and the fire lit, it creates an atmospheric space for more formal adult entertaining.

45 communal sitting rooms

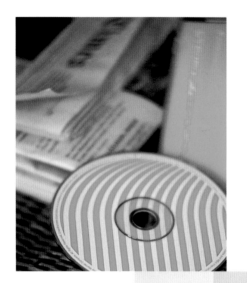

Kids love a designated playroom where they can keep their toys and play with friends. And grown-ups like them too, because they can shut a door on the mess! As children grow up, a properly planned playroom can easily evolve into a teenage den or even a media room. So furnish it early on with great storage, practical surfaces and enough technology to cope with media leisure. Add cosy seating, and grown-ups will want to chill out in there too.

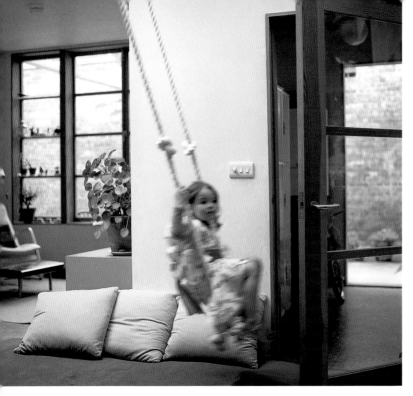

A designated playroom helps contain the sea of paraphernalia that comes with kids. There are dolly buggies and sit-on cars, then sports kit and art materials, not to mention the piano or football table. For parents, it can be a relief that these won't stray all over the house, and for children it's nice not to have to tidy away games in progress every night. It's also comforting for children to have a space they can call their own, particularly if bedrooms are shared. Later on, furnished with a desk and computer, a playroom becomes a place for homework. For older families, a home entertainment, or media room, is an increasingly popular option. In here, everything from the television and DVD player to the stereo system and Playstation can be smartly concealed and easily accessed.

Family homes rarely have rooms to spare, but however short of space you are it's worth considering if room functions can be switched. A designated den makes for more spacious, tranquil

LEFT AND OPPOSITE ABOVE: In a relaxed live/play space, younger kids will appreciate fun extras like a swing or punchbag or fold-away equipment like an easel or teepee. Install them beside the main traffic area, with cushions and a rug close by.

OPPOSITE BELOW: Allocate a separate tabletop or shelf to the kids, so drawing or homework needn't be cleared away when supper is ready. Overhead storage, or baskets clipped to one side, hold essentials.

BELOW: Experiment with novel ways to display kids' artworks, such as a wall-mounted clothes line and pegs.

living quarters elsewhere. Could two children share a bedroom, freeing up space for a playroom? If the kitchen contains an eating zone, could the dining room become a media room? What about a loft conversion, or the cellar? A conservatory extension is ideal for a playroom, because it is light and has outdoor access, as is a garden gazebo, wired and plumbed – perfect for noise control!

If a separate room isn't an option, then try to demarcate a play or chill-out zone within the family living space. For tinies, allocate floor space within the kitchen (safely away from the cooking area) so you can keep a close eye on them. Older children might appreciate a nook for table football, a basketball hoop on a first-floor landing, or even a small climbing wall, for the very brave! Make the boundaries clear. In a contemporary kitchen, different-coloured lino squares, a padded mattress or gym mats could mark out the kids' space. Alternatively, use freestanding storage units to divide off an area. In open-plan apartments or lofts, a mini maze is lots of fun.

OPPOSITE: Get the best use out of a designated playroom by keeping storage streamlined to free up maximum floor space. If kids are musical, this is the place to keep the piano or drums. Also consider table football, snooker, or plastic play equipment, such as a toddler's kitchenette. The less furniture there is, the more useful the room is for impromptu parties.
LEFT: Don't feel constrained to keep everything child-sized, as the best dens will appeal to grown-ups too. Choose squashy beanbags, a wall-size blackboard, or a big chill-out sofa.
ABOVE: Aim for easy-access storage, but fit a few doors so the worst mess can be instantly concealed.

OPPOSITE AND ABOVE: In a traditional playroom, keep things simple, with white walls and wooden floors, and let the toys – dolls' things, cars and trucks – create the decorative impact. Allow kids the creative freedom to display everything from their favourite paintings to postcards, memorabilia or photos. Allocate wall space or special shelves or provide a few bowls for favourite things to be grouped together.

LEFT: Invest in one large armoire or wardrobe into which everything can be tidied away. It could also be wired to hold the playroom TV and video.

THIS PAGE AND OPPOSITE: The computer is as much part of a family's leisure activities as the TV, so plan for its presence. If it is permanently on display, choose a colourful design, and remember to leave room for the printer. Computer play is a solitary pursuit, so pick a quiet corner and add good task lighting. Nearby storage means that paper for printing, computer games and other accessories can be neatly stowed away.

When decorating a designated playroom, approach it with a creative spirit and ask the kids what they'd like – after all, this is their space. Painted walls are practical and it can be fun to have a wall or two in jolly colours the children have chosen. Look out for kids' paint ranges, which include sparkly and magnetic paint options, and choose gloss paint for woodwork, as it's easy to wipe down. Fit one wall with a metal board and magnets, and consider a large blackboard, or blackboard paint on cupboard fronts. Older children might like to customize their space. Provide them with a 2-metre-square canvas (from art shops) and let them paint it with their own design, to fill one wall.

In the playroom, as in the kitchen, practical flooring is essential to withstand rowdy games and messy play. Don't choose sisal, as it's uncomfortable to lie on and hard to clean. Go for painted floorboards, rubber or lino. The latter can be cut into myriad patterns, from camouflage print to abstract flowers.

While a playroom would be no fun without some scaled-down pieces of furniture, such as little tables and chairs, plan larger pieces with growing-up in mind. Choose an adult-size sofa and install built-in desktops on a rack system, so the level can be raised as children grow. Likewise, swivel desk chairs should be height-adjustable, particularly important as children sit for longer hours doing homework. Plan capacious storage that fills an entire wall, and teenagers will still be using it long after the

LEFT AND OPPOSITE: When the family sitting room doubles as a media room, and your kids are tiny, consider wall-mounting the TV to keep it out of harm's way. Likewise, the video and CD could be concealed in built-in units. BELOW: Plan ample storage to keep videos, DVDs and CDs in order, and keep it low level to make it easy for kids to find what they want, and for older children to stay tidy. Tailor-made drawers or alcoves are one solution; alternatively, look out for plastic racks that can be fitted within larger storage units.

playroom has become a den. In a playroom, toy storage is all about instant access, so go for built-in shelves stacked with crates, or an open cube system. Flexible freestanding options include a plan chest (good for storing artwork) or a television/video unit on wheels.

As kids get older, they (and you) might want more than just a television in the playroom. Today's family home is increasingly infiltrated by media of all types, including satellite television, computer games and DVD players. It can make sense to devote an entire room to home entertainment. Options range from a trendy wall-mounted plasma-screen television to a motorized cinema screen for movies. There can be surround-sound emerging from concealed speakers, CD players, even a special socket so children can safely

LEFT: A playroom is the ideal spot for displaying family snaps, sports trophies or other memorabilia.
ABOVE AND BELOW: Keep furnishings ultra-practical, so that TV dinners or teenage nights in can take place with minimum fuss, and an upholstered stool won't wilt beneath muddy trainers. Leather, vinyl or washable loose covers are cosy yet practical choices.

plug in the Playstation. The beauty of such rooms is that all the technology is controlled by one automated operating system, hidden in a cupboard. It's not cheap to install, and you will need to decorate the room from scratch once the cabling is in place. But there are huge advantages. Teenagers can play loud music, or watch DVDs you'd rather not share, while you reclaim a tranquil sitting room. And, precisely because the technology must be fitted by specialists, there will be no trailing wires and fewer television sets elsewhere in the house.

Decorate a media room with relaxation in mind. There should be enough seating to accommodate family and friends. Low-level daybeds or modular seating systems upholstered in denim, velvet or chenille set the right tone, as do battered leather armchairs. Alternatively, consider floor-level seating like big floor cushions and a rug to sprawl on. Pay attention to lighting. If overhead low-voltage lights are necessary, add a dimmer switch, and try to include a fun, wall-mounted light. Don't forget a good task light, too, if the computer is located in here.

For successful viewing, a room needs good light control. Fit windows with blackout blinds and play up the mood with deep wall colours, from caramel to olive. Alternatively, experiment with fabric-covered walls, which are good for light and noise control. If the room is predominantly for teenagers, make it fun for them. Choose large-scale mural wallpaper – an alpine scene or enlarged graphic images – or sparkly wallpaper. Make the media room a funky hideaway and whatever's on, everyone will be in there watching.

LEFT, ABOVE AND BELOW: Position the television according to the ages of your family. Kids love sprawling on the floor, so choose a TV on an adjustable stand, set into a fireplace or – if choosing a plasma screen – wall-mounted at a low level. Have fun with media room furnishings, as kids and adults alike enjoy splashes of bright colours, either as rugs cushions or upholstery.

kids' rooms
shared bathrooms
parents' rooms

peaceful zones

'It's so important for a child to be able to shut his or her bedroom door and have solitude. Younger children need that for imaginative play, and privacy is even more important for teenagers.'

KATE, MOTHER

'It's good to have my own room – a place where I can take my friends, away from everyone else and listen to music.'

JOSH, AGE 15

'Our bathroom has a huge Japanese-style bath, so we bathe together – it's both meditative and fun.'

CECILIE, MOTHER

kids' rooms

From babyhood to the teenage years, a child's room is a tranquil retreat, somewhere to sleep and dream. Respect your children's need for privacy and quiet. Remember too that for kids, a bedroom represents the one space they can truly make their own, filled with all their favourite things. While young ones need a watchful decorative eye, allow teenagers flexibility. Let them experiment and make mistakes – they have to sleep in there, not you!

When family living space is properly planned, with storage equally distributed around the house, the kids' rooms will benefit too. Instead of battling with clutter, you (and they) have the chance to create a personalized area where kids feel relaxed playing or entertaining their friends. Children's lives are busier than ever, so it's essential to help them wind down at night. For younger ones, the answer is to keep computers and televisions out of the bedroom. For teenagers (who may insist on them), concentrate instead on promoting a relaxed ambience. Whatever the age, remember that the best bedrooms provide a truly peaceful place to sleep.

If you have several children, allocate bedrooms fairly, as size does matter. Babies will be happy in a cosy boxroom, and teenagers won't mind either, tending to value privacy over square metres. It's in the middle years that children will benefit from greater floor space, so their room can double as a playroom. Consider location. Tinies will gain comfort from sleeping right next to the master bedroom (and you will appreciate a shorter trip in the middle of the night). By contrast, older kids will positively prefer a corridor between you and them, or even sleeping on another floor. An attic hideaway is the best noise-control solution for teenage music-lovers.

Before considering the decor, plan the storage space, as no child will be able to sleep peacefully if there's mess all over the floor. For flexibility, combine a variety of different options. Built-in cupboards, with plenty of adjustable shelves, are ideal, but also provide some open shelves, for books and displaying treasures. Sturdy hooks, with some hangers, are essential, so

OPPOSITE: When they are little, same-sex siblings may prefer sharing a low double bed, with two duvets, rather than beds at opposite ends of the room. Or consider two divans, side by side, which can be separated to give independence in later years.

ABOVE RIGHT: Combine proper cupboard storage with easy-access shelves, so toddlers can find their favourite things.
RIGHT: Lighting is crucial. Fit windows with blinds or curtains lined with blackout material, and put overhead lights on a dimmer switch.

RIGHT AND OPPOSITE: A custom-built bed maximizes space in a small room, and adds quirky charm. And little children are less likely to fall out of beds that are boxed in (opposite) or have high sides. Sketch a style or amass tear-sheets, then get a carpenter to build a simple frame in MDF and paint it in a jolly shade. Storage can be incorporated in the form of under-bed drawers, or consider a platform bed with low cupboards beneath. Younger children will always appreciate a bed tucked against the wall or into a corner for added security.

busy kids can hang up clothes quickly if they don't make it to the wardrobe. Teenagers may prefer a chrome, shop-style hanging rack or a low, denim-covered storage unit in place of a chest of drawers. Kids of every age need easy-access floor-level storage, from plastic crates on castors to metal dustbins, so shoes and toys can be quickly sorted out and tidied away.

For babies, the bedroom should be styled as simply as possible. This not only guarantees a tranquil space for sleep, but allows for the child to slowly grow into the room, amassing possessions along the way. Even at the tiny baby stage, it pays to take a more long-term view when you are kitting out the bedroom. At first, the most essential piece is the cot, but within two years, along with the changing table, this will be redundant. In contrast, other key basics, including a chest of drawers, plenty of storage or shelves, and a comfortable feeding then reading chair, should last throughout a child's time at home. Look out for funky extras to please pre-school toddlers, such as a miniature table and chairs or a blow-up armchair.

LEFT: Long before the homework years, get younger children into good habits by installing a table in the bedroom, stocked with pens and paper or a globe. Choose from contemporary mini tables and chairs, or look out for retro finds to mix and match.

BELOW LEFT: Some children quickly tire of particular patterns on a duvet or curtains, so plan a plain white bedroom, from walls to bedlinen, then encourage them to add character with bold artworks, cheery strings of bunting or a changing monthly seasonal theme.

Decoratively speaking, it's fun to use colour in a baby's room, so don't fret about choosing peaceful shades (a blackout blind is what really promotes sleep). For a contemporary look, try painting blocks of solid colour on two walls, while keeping the others white, or spray-paint a built-in storage unit in bright pink or orange. Wool carpet or rubber tiles in acid shades are an energizing, practical choice. If you're artistic, attempting a large-scale mural is fun, but pick a unisex theme, such as the rainforest, so it's suitable for siblings sharing later on. Do use pattern, as little ones relish it. Steer clear of patterned wallpaper, which dates quickly, and pick printed bedlinen or cushions. These can be altered as tastes change. Whimsical prints, from animals to fruits, or abstracts, from dots to stripes, will please both sexes and endure beyond gimmicky kids' TV characters.

Small kids appreciate the fun of trendy, multi-functional furniture, so start with the bed. Always choose a full-size single bed, as kids quickly grow out of miniature styles. Bunk bed styles, in ready-to-paint MDF or minimal tubular steel, are perennial favourites, perhaps because they double up as a climbing frame! For girls, a simple wood or metal four-poster offers endless decorative opportunities – adorn it with muslin curtains, strands of beads or floral fairy lights. A low divan on giant castors, with plenty of underbed storage, is another fun option. The beauty of dual-purpose furniture is that it's space-saving and grows up with your child. A platform bed with a tabletop, bookshelf and chair slotted in underneath will be perfect for homework in later years, while a built-in alcove bed can be transformed into a grown-up daybed for teeny-bop girls.

LEFT, ABOVE AND BELOW:
Many older children are
enthusiastic collectors, be it
of toy soldiers or plastic
animals, so provide plenty
of display space. Wall-
mounted shelves or a low
worktop are good choices,
but consider too a panelled
cupboard, fitted with
chicken wire instead of
glass, or a series of wall-
mounted boxes, into which
everything from baby ballet
shoes to dried leaves and
conkers can be arranged.

OPPOSITE: Plan a child's workstation with the same care you would devote to an adult home office. Aim to make it comfortable and inspiring, so kids actively want to spend time there. Brightly coloured units, a flower-bedecked swivel chair or a pinboard fitted to cupboard doors are all popular additions. The desk should be positioned to get maximum benefit from natural light. Don't forget sufficient power points for a good task light and computer and a telephone line for the internet.
LEFT: If you have a playroom elsewhere in the house, keep things ultra-simple in a shared room, with barely more than a bed and adequate clothes storage.

Furniture needs alter radically at seven-plus. First, there's homework. Doing it at the kitchen table shouldn't be the only option: every child needs a quiet spot to study. Provide them with a roomy desk so they can spread out (or work with a friend) and a height-adjustable chair (or two), with a filing cabinet or storage crates beneath. Don't forget an internet phone socket if computer homework is likely. It's better to customize an adult work table than waste money on small kiddie-size desks. A built-in MDF worktop can be spray-painted in bright gloss, while a trestle table can be jazzed up with a trendy plastic swivel chair. If space permits, devote an entire wall to a purpose-built storage and desk unit, with cubbyholes for everything from CDs to books. Now's also the time to provide girls with a dressing table, for all that sparkly jewellery, or boys with a low craft table.

These days children are so style-conscious that from three upwards they'll want to have a say in decorative decisions. Provided you've chosen plain flooring and a simple white blackout roller blind or Venetian blind, kids can customize and change

THIS PAGE: Match kids' rooms stylistically to the rest of the house. If you prefer antique or junk-shop styles, have fun searching for quirky furniture children will enjoy too. Fun bed choices include *bateau lits*, a Victorian iron four-poster or a school dormitory style. All will last a child into their late teens, and can be made more grown-up with sophisticated bedlinen.
OPPOSITE: Give kids a chance to get into good grooming habits by supplying a dressing table for girls or a chunky chest of drawers for boys, plus a mirror positioned low enough for them to use.

their rooms with regularity. Windows can be hung with ready-made curtains, in any fabric from denim to lurex, and walls repainted in a fresh colour each year, provided your children are handy with a paintbrush! Older kids may like to consider wallpapers specifically aimed at the pre-teen market, from raised glitter hearts to abstract circles.

Encourage children to mix patterns rather than using matching co-ordinates. On the bed, printed duvet covers, in patterns ranging from gingham to stylized flowers, can be teamed with fleece blankets in *faux* leopard or Mexican stripes. Look out for fun extras such as a camouflage cushion cover for boys or a satin-effect eiderdown for girls. There's a good reason for keeping pattern to accessories rather than emblazoned all over the walls or floor. In larger families, it's likely children will swap bedrooms or decide to share, then return to the original set-up. Personalize a bedroom too much, and that freedom is curtailed.

If kids share permanently, help them maintain privacy and create a small space of their own. Little ones will enjoy bunks or beds close together, but older children may prefer to sleep at opposite ends of a room, with a dividing partition.

ABOVE, LEFT TO RIGHT: Kids love to personalize their own bedrooms, and this is particularly crucial in a large family. Let them paint their names on the bedroom door, add a monogrammed cushion to each bed, or – in a shared room – individualize their space with a specific theme, from underwater to a sports motif.

RIGHT: Some girls will want to mark the transition from childhood to the teenage years by opting for a simple, plain space with a few funky accessories, but the all-white minimalist look only works for super-tidy individuals.

OPPOSITE: Keep things simple for teenage boys, too. Easy-to-use underbed storage, a no-nonsense bed and utility bedlinen, from camouflage prints to a striped wool blanket, will be appreciated.

Flexible freestanding options include a large bookcase or an MDF screen on castors. A permanent partition wall can be made more sociable if portholes are cut into it at intervals. Sliding doors dividing the two areas, perhaps painted with blackboard paint or fitted with cork pinboards, also help personalize areas.

Don't panic when children hit the teenage years. The key is to hand over decorative responsibility to them (within limits!). Get them to plan a scheme on a budget – artistic individuals can sketch out the look too. Try to be open-minded about colour choice. No doubt boys will want to replace the cheerful brights of earlier years with moody navy and khaki, while girls will plump for bordello pink and black, but adolescents need to experiment and develop their tastes. Take them shopping for funky accessories, from velvet curtains to a wacky lampshade – this may be just the encouragement they need to make them proud of their space and keep it tidy.

THIS PAGE AND OPPOSITE, ABOVE RIGHT: Teenagers value their privacy, so a loft conversion bedroom, a four-poster bed hung with curtains or an alcove bed will all be popular. Don't forget a Keep Out sign for the door! Older kids may opt for more adult decorative schemes, which provide a soothing background for sleep or study: consider all-white or bleached tones of blue, grey or green. OPPOSITE, ABOVE LEFT AND BELOW: There are tasteful ways around dog-eared sports posters. Consider a wall-mounted football shirt or a bold painted canvas depicting a favourite sport.

There is a solution to poster-splattered walls. Come to an agreement that one wall only can be decorated any way they like (from spray-can graffiti to Warhol-style repeat photocopies) while the rest remains plain and unadorned. Alternatively, fit a giant metal pinboard with lots of magnets, so poster images are artfully contained. In a converted loft space, bare concrete or brick walls will be deemed the ultimate in cool.

The average teen room also doubles up as space for entertaining. If the room is tiny, a divan can be converted into a sophisticated daybed with the addition of a fitted loose cover and bolsters. If there's space, create a sitting area with vinyl pouffes or a foam mattress or futon, covered in hard-wearing denim – not only perfect for lounging on, but also useful for sleepovers. Invest in a few extras, such as a coffee table or a TV cabinet on wheels, and they'll never come downstairs again.

shared bathrooms

The family bathroom is undeniably one of the hardest-working rooms in the house. To cope with the endless stream of twice-daily ablutions, it needs excellent plumbing, a free-flowing layout and as many wash options as possible, from double basins to a power shower. Yet it's crucial to tread a fine line between practicality and beauty. For grown-ups, the bathroom must also be a place that visually and physically soothes at the end of a long, hard day.

More than ever we're a nation obsessed with cleanliness. The family bathroom has to withstand the early morning rush, splashy kids' bath times and the grown-ups' long, leisurely soak, not to mention teenagers endlessly sprucing themselves in the shower. Plan the bathroom well, and there's less likelihood of that clichéd queue outside the bathroom door.

We can't all have a huge bathroom, but with lots of people sharing, generous proportions do help. If there's only one tiny bathroom at home, consider moving it. This sounds a big upheaval but relocating the bathroom to a larger room can be well worth the expense and effort. Less radically, could you knock through to an adjacent toilet, or steal some space from a next-door bedroom? Sometimes, opting for one large bathroom with an additional small shower room is more functional than two tiny en suite bathrooms.

Think about location. If kids are small, it's essential that the bathroom is on the same level as their bedrooms, to make night-time toilet trips easier. Remember that plumbing can be noisy if you've

OPPOSITE: Plan streamlined storage so the bathroom isn't cluttered. A glass-fronted cabinet can be inset into the wall – with its 'invisible' frontage, it's less likely to attract small children's attention if medicines are stored inside. Wall-mounted basins, with towel holders below, are also helpful.

ABOVE: A shower can be incorporated into a family bathroom by stealing space at one end of the room and concealing it behind an internal wall.
BELOW: Innovative ways to link en suites to the master bedroom include a window-style aperture, (with shutters for privacy) or sliding or folding doors.

fitted power pumps to taps, so late-night baths or showers may disturb them. If this is the case, site the bathroom next to the master bedroom. Teenagers will appreciate a shower room close to their bedrooms, so consider that if you're planning a loft conversion. Older children consider it very grown-up to have their bedrooms plumbed with a small basin.

As parents, if you crave your own facilities, consider incorporating the main bathroom into the master bedroom. This is particularly effective in a loft space, or knocked-through, L-shaped bedrooms in a Victorian house. The arrangement works best when children are small, so they can bathe while you have

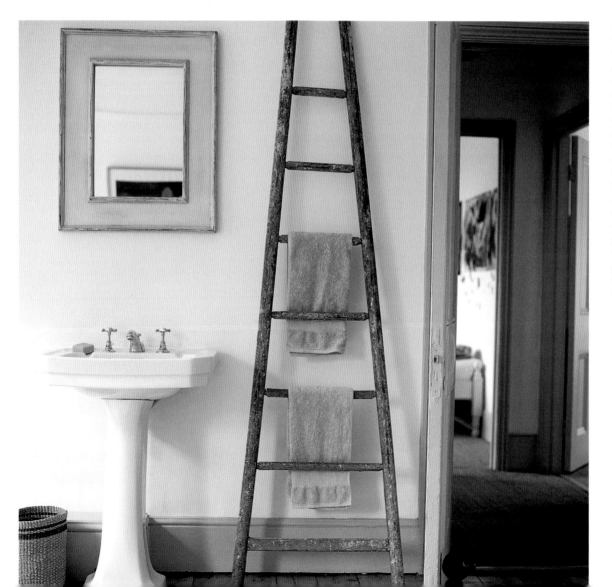

LEFT AND ABOVE LEFT: The bigger your family, the more towel space you need. In addition to a heated towel rail, consider fun extras such as an Oriental-style bamboo ladder or folding wooden or chrome racks. A coat-stand makes a great choice for towelling dressing gowns.
OPPOSITE: In a traditional bathroom, experiment with less conventional storage options. A distressed wooden trunk can be filled with spare towels, and a glass- or chicken-wire fronted cabinet makes a great display for attractive bath products, one shelf for each member of the family.

OPPOSITE LEFT, FROM ABOVE TO BELOW, AND RIGHT: Help everyone stay tidy by furnishing the bathroom with plenty of large hooks for cast-off clothes, and occasional baskets for toilet rolls, flannels or bathtime reading. In a large family, you might even consider numbered hooks to encourage order.

LEFT: It's possible to choose a sophisticated decorative scheme, whatever age the kids are. With a washable loose chair cover, and easy-to-wipe panelling, this all-white bathroom is both practical and beautiful.

a lie-in and there's lots of space for running around. As parents, you get the benefit of a roomy, light bathroom for relaxing in before bed (though fit sliding screens or double doors for privacy at night). The downside is you'll find little ones passing through your room on midnight trips to the toilet. Another solution is to formally separate the en suite bathroom, but make it large enough for all the family. The ideal combination is a separate children's shower room and toilet as well.

Less-than-perfect plumbing should be overhauled. It's vital for busy families to have piping hot water that won't run out after the first bath. If moving house, invest in a new, larger hot-water cylinder, but ensure that your boiler is powerful enough to keep it stocked. Power pumps will improve water flow from taps and the shower head. Include at least one heated towel rail on the hot water circuit, to avoid endlessly soggy towels. Alternatively, an electrical one can be switched on when needed. Think about underfloor heating, as it makes even chilly stone floors cosy.

Storage is crucial. If the airing cupboard is in the bathroom, it's the obvious place to store towels. Otherwise, opt for a slim freestanding unit, built-in shelves or deep drawers beneath a

vanity unit. Where do all the lotions and potions go? Allow the family one shelf above the basins for everyday bottles, from cleanser to aftershave, and wall-mount toothbrush-mugs, so small kids don't knock them over. Then insist that all remaining clutter is stowed away. Allocate an individual shelf or cupboard to each family member. A row of medicine-style cabinets or lockers looks trendy and neat. Inside one large cupboard, smaller containers can hold everything from hairbrushes to soaps. Don't forget a big laundry bin, and locate it in an obvious place, so kids actually use it.

When planning a bathroom from scratch, draw up a floor plan to scale and move around cut-outs of proposed sanitary ware. It's the only way to assure a free-flowing layout, allowing quick access to the toilet and basins in the morning. It will also help you make design choices. For example, if there's no room for a hinged shower door, plan a fixed sand-blasted screen. If possible, position the bath centrally rather than against the wall. It's easier to get at slippery small children, and may create a free corner where a chair can go.

When it comes to sanitary ware, nothing beats a big bath. Smaller siblings can share bathtime, and grown-ups enjoy the luxury too. Cast-iron styles often come in extra-deep or long proportions, and traditional rolltop baths are generously sized. Choose practical bath panels that won't spoil if splashed, such as painted MDF, laminate or sand-blasted glass lit from within with coloured lights. Centrally sited

OPPOSITE, TOP ROW: A traditional style of sanitary ware, teamed with a classic all-white scheme, makes the perfect family choice. It can be dressed up with pretty chandeliers, antique mirrors or giant scented candles to suit grown-ups, but looks equally at home furnished with kids' bathtime toys, or a distressed wooden stool for little ones to reach the basin.

OPPOSITE, BOTTOM ROW: Don't despair if the family bathroom is tiny. Look out for fittings that can double up, from a combined radiator and towel rail to a basin inset into a storage unit. If you've a family of teenagers, is a bath really essential? A great power shower, which takes up less room, may be a better alternative.

BELOW, LEFT TO RIGHT: Choose taps and fittings with practicality in mind. A generous-sized spout will fill a bath quicker than two conventional bath taps, while basin mixer taps reduce the likelihood of younger kids scalding their hands.

mixer taps are more comfortable for children, and take up even less room if wall-mounted. And add an efficient shower head attachment, so hair-washing is possible even if the shower cubicle is in use.

Two basins will speed up morning ablutions. Wall-mounted ceramic styles take up less room than traditional pedestal basins, or double up on facilities by fitting a basin on a stainless-steel stand, so towels can hang below. Alternatively, consider counter-sinking two basins into a built-in storage unit with cupboards beneath. In a contemporary bathroom, a purpose-built long, shallow, tiled or ceramic trough is a streamlined option. If the toilet is situated in the main bathroom, it's essential to have at least one other elsewhere in the house. And however sociable a bathroom you've planned, don't forget a lock on the door – well out of the reach of tiny fingers.

A shower is essential in a household containing teenagers. If possible, install a separate shower cubicle within the family bathroom, rather than making do with a showerhead over the bath. Squeeze in a separate shower room elsewhere at home – even in the utility room or cellar – and you will immediately triple the family's washing options. Invest in the best shower you can afford, with a fixed shower head and a pump for excellent water pressure.

In a separate shower room, go for a wet-room style with tiled walls and a floor drain, so that younger kids can pile in together instead of squeezing into a small cubicle. Keep things streamlined with wall-mounted soap and shampoo dispensers. Flooring must be non-slip.

BELOW, LEFT TO RIGHT: If space is tight, then investigate alternative options, including an extra-small bath, a sitz-style bath/shower, or one that is custom-built to fit the space and lined with tiles. A small bath can be comforting for little ones, but consider growing children and adults' needs too by combining it with a shower option. OPPOSITE: A wet-room-style shower, with floor drain, is quick, practical and fun for kids.

OPPOSITE: Consider privacy in the family bathroom. No-one wants to look directly at the toilet, and even little kids can be surprisingly prudish if sharing with older siblings. Conceal the toilet behind a discreet partition, or provide a sliding sand-blasted glass door.

ABOVE AND LEFT: If the bathroom is an odd shape, consider building bathing facilities to fit the available space. Mosaic tiles fit the tightest corners and make a great decorative choice, as they come in myriad bright colours, and can be used to individualize a room with unusual motifs and shapes.

Mosaic tiles or concrete are good options, but add a non-slip rubber or slatted wood mat on stone floors. Make the shower room fun and bright for the kids. Mosaic and ceramic tiles come in myriad strong colours, while cement can be inset with glitter mosaics or pebbles for the ultimate non-slip surface.

In contrast, the main bathroom needs a neutral colour scheme, as one minute it will be filled with bright bath toys, the next needed as a pre-party relaxation zone for teenagers or grown-ups. Paint walls in cool shades or choose a polished plaster finish or all-over tiling in pastel or white tiles – neutrals are soothing for everyone, and splashes are easily wiped down. Likewise, MDF panelling or tongue and groove, painted with eggshell, are practical options. Pick flooring that is safe but robust. Stone, wood or the ever-practical lino and rubber are all good choices and come in a variety of neutral shades. Control daylight with a simple roller blind, wooden shutters or sand-blasted-glass panels in the windows.

Because the family bathroom is shared by all ages, try to include special treats everyone will enjoy. A cosy armchair, loose-covered in towelling, is the perfect spot for little ones cuddling up after a bath or teenagers painting their toe-nails. Provide plenty of fluffy towels, perhaps colour-coding them for each member of the family. There should be a mirror that everyone can see into (and if kids are tiny, provide a sturdy stool), with good lighting for make-up. If you've a family of boys, add a shaver socket and extendable mirror. A chrome trolley, to hold magazines and comics, and a radio – so that everyone can sing along in the bath – should keep the whole family happy.

OPPOSITE AND RIGHT:
If a parents' en suite bathroom is to be shared by all, great storage is essential. Include space for toiletries and clean towels, not to mention cleaning materials, toilet rolls and medicine cabinet essentials. Look out for extra-large towel rails (right) to accommodate multiple towels. Make the family bathroom cosy for everyone. Underfloor heating is ideal, while lighting on a dimmer and a low bath that small children will find easy to get into are desirable.

parents' rooms

Parents deserve a tranquil and relaxing bedroom, a retreat from the rigours and noise of family life. Children need to understand it's a private place too. To create the ultimate adult switch-off zone, plan the master bedroom with cool colours and minimal furniture in mind. And don't forget to include the little luxuries so often edited out of a practical, family-friendly home. This is your space, so fill it with all the things you love best.

No adult, once a parent, will ever view the master bedroom in quite the same way again. It's no longer just a place to get dressed and to sleep. When your children are young, it's their first port of call from as early as daybreak, a focus for imaginative games, quiet cuddles and TV-watching in the parental bed. And while on weekends you won't see older children for dust, it's still a sanctuary for them during times of illness or for evening chats. Yet perhaps its greatest significance for time-pressed parents is that it's a retreat, a place for me-time and for winding down.

If planning a family home from scratch, consider the potential of each bedroom before choosing your own. Many parents pick the largest room out of convention, but this may not be the best strategy. Think five years ahead – how will family life have moved on? It would be a shame to kit out a luxurious en suite shower room off the master bedroom, only to find two years later that siblings need a bigger room to share – in other words, yours! Could you bag a room under the eaves, with the potential for a walk-in wardrobe, or would it be better divided into two small rooms plus shower room for soon-to-be teenagers?

Privacy is important. No-one wants to ban kids from the bedroom, but it's good for them to understand that, just as you respect their rooms, so they should respect yours. This division

may be simply achieved in a flat by locating your bedroom at one end of the corridor and the children's at the other. If building a house, and there's the space, create a 'buffer' zone between the bedroom door and the room where you sleep. A large room can be divided into a 'suite' of bathroom, bedroom and tiny dressing room, all leading off a short corridor that's accessed by one door.

Sometimes the parents' room opens directly off the main living space, and becomes part of it during the day. This is common in an open-plan single-level area or in a small flat, where every square centimetre counts. Create privacy with sliding doors in sand-blasted glass or painted MDF, or more traditional folding or double doors. All these options aid in noise control if the kids rise before you do. In a loft space, create cosy cubicle rooms for the children at ground level,

LEFT AND OPPOSITE: Whatever age your children are, it's worth considering the issue of privacy. So think about access routes to the bedroom. If the room is large, consider sectioning off the initial third (left), and furnish it with a small sofa or daybed, where children can congregate in the morning (or middle of the night) without totally disturbing your peace. A sliding door dividing the two will be less intimidating than a shut door for small kids.

OPPOSITE: The older children get, the more likely it is you'll reclaim your bedroom as a sanctuary. Floor space once necessary for little ones playing can now be filled with useful extras, from a sofa to a writing table or bookcase. This is the time to indulge all those decorative whims you've held back on for so long. An all-white bedroom creates the ultimate relaxation zone.

RIGHT: Enjoy making a decorative focus out of family photographs, which may be casually grouped together, as here, or hung to cover an entire wall.

then build a separate mezzanine level as a sleeping platform for grown-ups. A glass or steel balustrade around it, along with an enclosed staircase, are safety essentials if the children are small.

In the parental bedroom, carefully chosen minimal furniture will go a long way to keeping your mood serene, as well as freeing up floor space for active kids. If you have little ones who like to cuddle up in bed with you, consider investing in a king-size bed, so everyone has enough space. It's a good idea to include a small sofa. Children can perch here for early-morning TV-viewing while you snooze, or crash on it at night if feeling lonely. Alternatively, choose a sofa bed. If you don't have a spare room, guests can sleep in the kids' rooms, while the children use the sofa bed. And don't forget a bedside table, stacked with all the books you never get to read during the day.

The master bedroom also needs great storage so tired parents can quickly put away their own stuff at night. In a contemporary interior, a wall of fitted flush cupboards, painted to match the walls, hides everything. A pretty armoire or linen press are more traditional options. Make good use of chain-store storage fittings and kit out the inside with hanging rails, shelves and baskets for smaller items. The easier it is for you to tidy up, the less likely you are to drop a special dress on the floor late at night, only to find it fashioned into a 'tent' in the morning.

Think of your bedroom as a second private sitting room. Yes, family life is sociable, but as children grow up, they no longer go to bed at 8pm and will share most evenings with you, so it's nice to know you can retreat to your bedroom, good book in hand.

ABOVE, RIGHT AND OPPOSITE:
If you have rules about
kids coming into the
bedroom, make them
clear from an early age,
so everyone knows the
limits. Guidelines might
include no jumping on the
bed, not dragging
the duvet off and not
investigating the contents
of the wardrobe
(particularly in the case of
teenagers!). But let them
enjoy the luxuries you've
chosen to surround
yourself with, too.
Children will enjoy a bit
of grown-up glamour, be
that a glittery canvas,
touchy-feely textures on
the bed or a dressing
table with adjustable
mirrors and several
tempting little drawers.

ABOVE LEFT AND OPPOSITE: Given that the parental bedroom is all about relaxing, treat yourself to comfortable, even indulgent furnishings. Pile the bed high with feather pillows, invest in a good-quality mattress and choose a padded fabric headboard to make the most of any (very occasional) lie-ins. It's a good idea to have a selection of blankets as well as a conventional cotton-covered duvet, so you can all enjoy a Sunday morning tucked and wrapped, watching TV in bed.

ABOVE RIGHT: There are many advantages to deciding to site the parental bedroom in a loft. Quite apart from great natural light, there's the noise factor – no-one thundering past your bedroom on the stairs, and no patter of tiny feet overhead when you're trying to stay asleep.
RIGHT: If there's no room to squeeze in a comfy sofa, an occasional chair, even in the tiniest of bedrooms, is still ideal for laying out tomorrow's clothes, helping a child get dressed or impromptu night-time chats.

Add a small television, and there will be no more arguments about who watches what. Think carefully about the atmosphere you want to create. Fit dimmer switches on wall-mounted lights by the sofa and bed. Build in a stereo system if you can. Be indulgent. This is your private space, so if you want to fill a wall with your kids' artwork and family photos for contemplation in bed, do so.

The way you decorate the bedroom will crucially affect its ambience. It's refreshing to choose a moody colour scheme – muted off-pastels, neutrals, or exotic shades like damson or chartreuse – in contrast to the whites and clear colours so typical of a family home. Experiment with abstract or metallic wallpapers, or more romantic *toile de Jouy*. And don't be afraid to indulge in luxurious textures, even if you do have small children. Silk curtains and velvet cushions are perfectly possible, so long as the kids are taught to treat them with respect. Better still, hunt out satin eiderdowns or woollen throws that are washable, or at least dry-cleanable. And be warned. All children, from toddlers to teenagers, are as tuned-in to luxury as we are. Blink twice and that devore velvet throw will be on its way upstairs, en route to a small person's bedroom.

outdoors

storage

traffic areas

practical zones

'The kids know there's a place for everything in the house. It's easier for them, because they know where to find things, and good for me – because I hate to tidy up!'

LENA, MOTHER

'Keep the right stuff in the right places. We can just reach under the kitchen benches and get to the Play-doh, rather than having to run upstairs to the kids' bedrooms.'

SIMON, FATHER

'Storage and more storage! While the benefits of an open-plan space are that kids can play everywhere, I want to be able to tidy everything away at the end of the day.'

CLAIRE, MOTHER

outdoors

Families need an outdoor area, however tiny, for congregating at weekends or on long summer evenings. Even in winter, it's good to encourage the kids to get outside while you keep up with the gardening. Where there's a varied age span, your outdoor space must offer flexibility. There should be a play area for small children, active space for older kids and a relaxing spot where grown-ups and teenagers can read or snooze in comfort.

TOP LEFT AND OPPOSITE: Create an indoor/outdoor room for family use, and it will rarely be empty. Guard against a variable climate by choosing a space that offers some protection from the elements. A conservatory extension or patio with permanent roof and one or two fixed side walls are both good options. Furniture choices can be more varied if a space is sheltered. Consider rattan, bamboo or upholstered styles – more comfortable than conventional garden chairs. LEFT: The more seating choices around the house and garden, the better, from a balcony with rockers to a decked dining area.

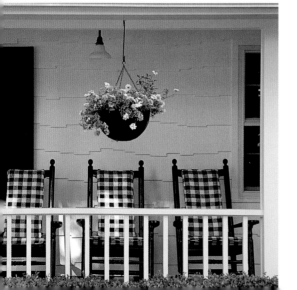

The great outdoors is a vital extension to your family living space. We can't all enjoy big gardens, but when the sun comes out and the back door is open, even the tiniest patio comes into its own. Younger children are naturally attracted outside, needing little more than a stick or slug to entertain them, while computer-game-obsessed older siblings need a little more encouragement. What would make outdoors enjoyable for them? The simple addition of a football area or basketball hoop might do the trick. You may even discover a burgeoning gardener, in need of an experimental flowerbed.

Think about outdoor access. For smaller children, it's ideal if the kitchen/playroom opens directly onto the garden, so they can wander in and out under a watchful parental eye. In a contemporary home, floor-to-ceiling glass sliding doors, or those designed to fold back on themselves, will instantly double the available play space. In a more traditional home, French windows create a similar effect. For grown-ups and teenagers, consider the appeal of a planked 'deck'. Traditionally sited between indoors and an expanse of lawn, a deck is the perfect spot for lounging, so equip it with a rocking chair or (if the deck is covered with an awning) upholstered bench seats.

RIGHT: There are advantages to high enclosing walls in a small city garden: they can protect against flying footballs, provide privacy and control noise. Prevent tall walls from overpowering a space and maximize on light by painting walls in reflective pale colours or obscuring them with an energetic, robust flowering creeper.

BELOW RIGHT: Everyone appreciates a cooling water feature, but if kids are small fit a protective cover for safety.
OPPOSITE: A playhouse needn't ruin an urban garden. Be inspired by the style of your house to create a purpose-built structure. Cement walls can be decorated with pebbles or handprints in abstract patterns.

Eating outdoors *en famille* is wonderfully sociable. Make it easy by having a table and chairs permanently set up, as impromptu lunches are less appealing if furniture must be moved first. Good-quality garden furniture designed to withstand the elements will last for more than a decade. Hardwood, aluminium, cast iron and plastic are all good choices. Pick as large a table as possible, to accommodate any extra guests. Great extras include a big sun umbrella, a barbecue and – the ultimate luxury – an outdoor heater for chillier nights.

When outdoor space is limited, it's important to combine practicality with good looks. Take the ages of your kids into account when choosing surfaces. If there are boys circling on bikes, forget grass – a tiny patch will soon become a mudbath. Instead, consider limestone paving or concrete, the ultimate roller-skating surface. Tiny children likely to take a tumble will fare better with decking. Concrete or brick walls, painted in strong Mediterranean shades or reflective white, can withstand repeated bashings from a football. If you have little ones, or more considerate teenagers, then woven willow or bamboo fence panels look good. Don't cut down on activity space by adding deep flowerbeds. Instead, group plants in containers, and ask the garden centre to recommend child-friendly species.

BELOW: Whatever age your children, accept that the garden will be infiltrated with equipment, from sit-on cars to scooters, bikes and skateboards. Either include a shed, for quick tidy-ups, or a covered outdoor 'store', in modern stainless steel for urban spaces, or seasoned hardwood in traditional gardens. These can be softened with climbers or made funky with strings of plastic beads.

Having children needn't mean the end of a beautifully planned garden. For a start, most kids enjoy the process of gardening, and will appreciate the chance to grow vegetables they can eat, flowers to pick for their bedrooms and undergrowth to rummage in. Try to choose fast-growing shrubs or ground-cover plants that can be trained to conceal the kids' play area, and if there's room, do allow for an area of tall, robust grasses, or a thicket of bamboo, which makes play much more fun.

Don't discount play equipment just because a space is small. Many high-street shops produce smaller-scale climbing frames designed for urban gardens, while older kids will enjoy a wall-mounted basketball hoop or pop-up goalposts. A small trampoline can be squeezed into a corner, but position it over a sunken area, filled with woodchips, if there's stone flooring elsewhere. If reclaiming the garden for adult barbecues is important, pick foldaway play equipment, and stash it in a small shed or storage bunker. Planning a garden from scratch allows for tasteful solutions. Consider an inset sandpit with a flush cover to match the decking, or a playhouse designed in the same materials as the walls/fence, so it seamlessly blends in.

If you have the luxury of a large garden, divide up the space with multiple activities in mind. Older, active children benefit from space for football or other ball games, but no-one wants to view scuffed turf. Position the kickabout zone at the end of the garden, and screen it from the house using trellising, covered with a fast-growing creeper, or by planting large shrubs and flowering trees to conceal the area behind.

Provide an array of outdoor activities the whole family can enjoy. Specialist mail-order catalogues sell garden games from giant building blocks to chess, then there are the classics, such as croquet or quoits. Tomboys of either sex will enjoy a sturdy rope and tyre securely fastened to a tree branch.

ABOVE: If possible, provide access to the street directly from the garden – consider fitting a new door into a garden wall if necessary – so that active kids arriving or departing on bikes or roller skates don't tread mud through the house.

RIGHT: In multifunctional family living spaces where kids are moving constantly in and out, pick furniture that looks good in both areas. Metal café-style furniture, low-slung plastic chairs and hardwood benches are good examples.

OPPOSITE: Converted warehouse homes often boast substantial outdoor space, though it may be impossible to transform this into a leafy oasis. Instead, play up the industrial aspect with concrete flooring, a wooden bench on chains and a skateboard ramp.

Also consider the option of larger outdoor play equipment. Specialist companies sell modular climbing frames that can be added to with ropes, scramble nets or slides. They are not cheap, but will entertain your kids for years, and are often manufactured in hardwoods to blend with the garden. Older children will relish a treehouse or other retreat. It's cheaper to buy a wooden shed and customize the interior than splashing out on a gingerbread-style Wendy house that kids will soon grow out of. If the garden is large, a big shed, wired and plumbed, makes a great games room. Check planning restrictions first, though.

The older kids get, the more they value privacy – outdoors as well as in. Teenagers might want to study in the garden in the summer months and adults need an outdoor escape. So in addition to sun loungers, provide fold-up canvas deckchairs or director's chairs that can be carried to the bottom of the garden.

A big hammock will appeal to all age groups. More formal options include a painted wooden gazebo, a garden seat overhung with a creeper or an upholstered swing chair. A summerhouse provides excellent out-of-season storage for everything from umbrellas to cricket bats.

For inner-city-dwellers, the only chance of outdoor space may be upwards, on a roof terrace. If you have small kids, high fencing and easy access via a sturdy staircase are essentials. But while ball games are clearly out of the question, a paddling pool and sandpit can easily be accommodated. If you have older children, turn the roof terrace into a trendy oasis. Add a small water feature – a fountain or a trickle of water over pebbles (avoid ponds if kids are still small). Invest in some funky moulded-plastic outdoor furniture, lay a square of Astroturf and string the surrounding balustrade with outdoor fairy lights.

OPPOSITE AND THIS PAGE:
The average roof terrace tends to be small, but if possible it's still worth dividing up the available space to suit several different functions. Most important is a generous table and chairs, as large as the space will allow. Also consider a trellis screen or bamboo or wicker fence panels to divide the eating area from a lounge spot in the sun. Exotic trees grown in containers can also create a pretty screen. Take time to plan your outdoor lighting – perfect for encouraging impromtu alfresco family meals.

Successful storage is the backbone of a smooth-running family home. Plan it carefully, and it will help reduce (if not prevent) the amiable chaos of family life. The key to good storage is to have more than you think is necessary, because kids' kit multiplies daily. And plan it with a decorative eye. Storage is essential in every room of the house, so it should look great as well as being practical.

THIS PAGE: Fitted storage needn't mean cupboards, and in a tiny boxroom, they may not even be an option. So think laterally. In this teenager's bedroom, a high platform bed accommodates plenty of drawer space. And for kids in a hurry, tidying clothes and possessions into low-level drawers is often more user-friendly than a classic hanging wardrobe. A wall-mounted TV shelf also saves on floor space.

OPPOSITE, ABOVE AND BELOW: Nothing beats open cube shelves for quick toy storage, and – in later years – for stowing away books and CDs. Ideally, fit some with cupboard doors so messier items can be concealed.

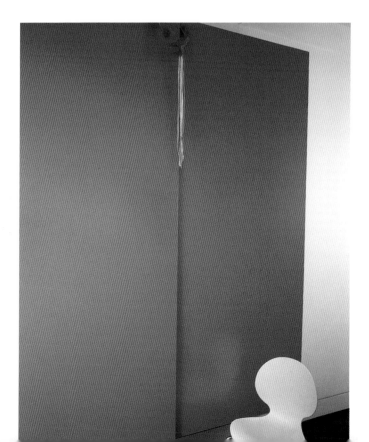

Nothing oils the wheels of family life better than a good storage system. Yet having ample, well-planned storage isn't just a question of owning a large house. A small living space works perfectly well if there's a place for everything. Family life isn't about having an immaculate home, but it isn't about living in chaos, either. It's harder to encourage kids to be neat if there's no designated storage for daily items. So be realistic. Aim for a storage system that allows for a good tidy-up when there's time, and basic organization when there isn't.

The bigger your family, the more clutter there will be. And from babyhood onwards, it multiplies. Rule number one is to have regular clear-outs, especially at Christmas and birthdays, when there's an influx of new stuff. Rule number two is to have a clear idea of what must be stored, and how frequently it's used. Get children (as well as grown-ups) to list their essential kit, from sports gear to CDs, camera equipment to picnic rugs. Examine the available storage through the whole house, from the cellar to the bedrooms, then create a masterplan of where everything

THIS PAGE AND OPPOSITE: In small spaces or traffic areas, it's imperative for storage to be 'invisible', so it won't get in the way of kids running around or interfere with a sleek, contemporary decorative impact. Flush doors with invisible touch catches, in a colour or finish to match the walls, are the ideal option. A carefully planned visual break in a run of cupboards can house a TV, computer, breakfast bar or worktop.

OPPOSITE, ABOVE FAR RIGHT: When storage conceals appliances such as a CD or video, the need for ventilation can be turned into a decorative asset. Punched metal, trellised MDF or cut-out circles look smart and are practical.

should go. Contemplating the house in its entirety, rather than room by room, means things get stored logically. Why keep your son's sports kit in his room, if it's easier to grab it in the hall?

Fitted made-to-measure storage is an investment, but pays vast practical dividends. In a large room, with space to spare, you can't beat an uninterrupted bank of wall-to-wall shelves. But it's still possible to be inventive when space is tight. In a small room, 'stealing' a depth of 50 cm across the width of one wall creates enough space for a wall of flush cupboards. Precisely because fitted storage is tailor-made, it maximizes the available space in the most awkward of corners, from bookshelves above a door to vertical shoe-racks under the stairs. It can also be as task- or object-specific as you like. A run of minimalist storage cupboards can house the kids' TV, a contemporary playroom bench can conceal toys beneath its lid, and bulky items – from the Hoover to the space-hopper – can be squeezed into understair cupboards.

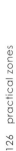

ABOVE LEFT AND RIGHT:
Storage must fit in with
your decorative style, so
if your look is more
traditional, pick simple
mirrored or panelled
freestanding armoires.
Rethink the way you use
classic pieces. A large
armoire might do better
service as a toy cupboard
in the kitchen, rather than
cluttering up a bedroom,
while a chest of drawers
on a roomy landing can
house extra bedding.
LEFT: Experiment with the
levels of shelving or open
storage, especially in a
small space. Shelves can

be run around a room
at ceiling height, hung
below a window, or
floor-mounted.
OPPOSITE, LEFT AND RIGHT:
Tall, thin shelving units
can serve kids' and
adults' needs alike.
Dangerous or precious
items that you'd rather
small children didn't
reach, or infrequently
used toys and books, can
be stored well out of the
way, while lower shelves
are devoted to everyday
necessities. A library
ladder can be a fun
addition for accessing
very tall shelves.

How do you want storage to look? In rooms where you entertain, or want to feel peaceful, always fit cupboard doors, so it doesn't matter if there's chaos lurking within. Flush-fitting doors painted or wallpapered to match walls will discreetly 'disappear', especially if fitted with invisible touch catches. For contrast, consider stainless steel, laminates or gloss-painted MDF, or in traditional homes, panelled door fronts. In playrooms or utility zones, open shelves or wall-mounted cube storage are ideal as they provide instant access for kids. Keep them neat by fitting them with smart containers in wicker, card or plastic.

If moving into a new house, don't rip out existing storage just because it looks dated. The original cupboard carcasses may be put to good use. Moulded doors can be replaced with perspex or sand-blasted glass, and shelves made more contemporary with the addition of a thick front edge. If you're staying put in an existing house, and can't afford fitted storage, consider off-the-shelf DIY options. They are inexpensive, and available in many finishes, from wood veneers to lacquer. These days, there's an array of unusual door handles that will customize cupboards further, but pick chunky versions if there are small kids around.

Not everyone wants sleek fitted storage. Freestanding pieces can move house with you, and have the potential to shift from one room to another as family needs alter. Regular furniture can also be customized. A beautiful armoire will be more user-friendly if fitted with many shelves, instead of a high hanging rail, while a low retro-style drinks cabinet could conceal the video. Kids will enjoy foraging in junk shops for a chest of drawers or bureau, which they can paint and customize for their room. Also consider inexpensive chain-store storage options, from a TV cabinet to shoe cupboards. And get inventive with budget

THIS PAGE AND OPPOSITE: The average family accumulates an amazing amount of 'stuff', but organizing everything by type, rather than by owner, can help. For example, decide that all books are shelved in the sitting room, all outdoor gear stashed in the cellar, and all CDs kept in the kitchen, rather than distributed around the house. The more you can compartmentalize storage, the better. Thus, shelves should be fitted with lots of baskets, the inside of a cabinet with sliding drawers and metal racks, and the backs of doors with multiple, rather than single, hooks. And keep a roomy easy-to-carry basket permanently at the bottom of the stairs. Encourage anyone going up – from little ones to grown-ups – to replace stray items on a regular basis, and that way no-one bears the brunt of a mass tidy-up.

plywood or galvanized metal storage cubes or stacking storage systems from high-street stores. Wall-mounted at unusual heights (from ankle level to above a window), or used in multiple quantities, they can look as chic as bespoke storage.

All storage systems work best if fitted with containers that hold smaller items. You can't go wrong with clear plastic crates and lidded containers, clearly labelled, so kids can see toys and equipment at a glance. Grown-ups might prefer rattan baskets, zinc containers or cardboard boxes, to hold everything from photos to Christmas decorations. Put kids' stuff on lower shelves and infrequently used items at the top. Don't clutter valuable cupboard space with out-of-season items. Banish them to the loft or the cellar. Make good use of ad hoc storage accessories, like wall-mounted CD, wine and magazine racks. If there's a space for everything, then everyone – even the laziest child – can be persuaded to put things away.

However good the storage system, it's vital to provide the whole family with the means for a rapid tidy-up when visitors are imminent or you have had enough of slowly encroaching chaos. Each room should have a basket, tucked out of sight, for magazines and toys. Hang hooks in bathrooms, halls and kitchens, for getting everything off the floor quickly. And invest in an attractive filing cabinet, in powder-coated steel, to keep family paperwork under control.

Every parent knows the exuberance with which children arrive home, dump their stuff in the hall and clatter up the stairs. All too often, these traffic areas don't get the attention they deserve. So treat such crucial spaces with respect. Fitted with robust surfaces and proper storage to keep them clutter-free, efficient traffic areas make for streamlined and safe family living. They can also become the most dramatic-looking areas of the house.

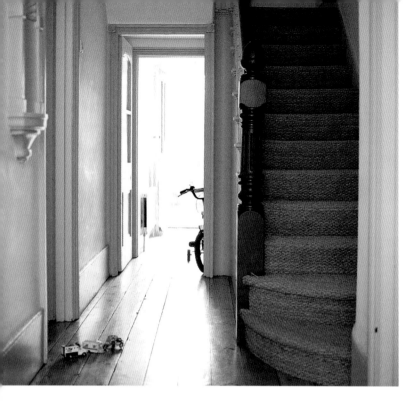

Every home needs an inviting hallway, to welcome family and visitors alike. So be strict with the kids about not dumping bags on the floor. Fit the walls with pegs at varying levels and several shoe racks, so hastily discarded gear can be immediately stowed. Wall-hang bikes on a pulley system, and fold buggies before storing beneath the stairs. If there's room, add a bench so kids can boot up comfortably, and school gear be left out for the morning. If there's no space for a traditional hall table, wall-mount a large letter rack by the front door, so post and school notices don't go astray, and add hooks for keys.

Stairs must be safe. If moving to a new house when kids are small, check there's no more than a 100mm gap between bannisters (the legal maximum) and replace any worn, slippery stair carpet. Where stairgates are essential, rather than buy ugly

OPPOSITE: Pay attention to entry and exit points, both practically and visually. Aesthetically, it's pleasurable for everyone entering to see through to a vista outdoors. If there's no such view, might a doorway be moved to allow for one, or French doors positioned at the rear so kids can run straight outdoors? If there's space, it's a good idea to locate a downstairs cloakroom close to the front or back door.

LEFT AND BELOW: In a contemporary space, solid plywood, toughened glass or metal mesh make sturdy alternatives to traditional bannisters and may be safer for small children to use.

BELOW LEFT AND OPPOSITE, RIGHT: In a big hall, one or two key pieces will set the decorative tone, but they must be practical too. A bench or upholstered sofa is useful for school kit, while a narrow hall table will hold all the paraphernalia.

BELOW RIGHT AND OPPOSITE, LEFT: Fitting built-in cupboards in an already narrow corridor hall may not be an obvious option, but the resulting storage will keep the precious remaining space clear.

white metal versions, get a carpenter to create a simple MDF design, then paint to match the décor. Good lighting is essential. Inserting a skylight above the stairwell can flood it with light. Side lights, on a dimmer, at intervals on the stairs, will provide a welcome home to late-arriving teenagers. Low-voltage lights inset at ankle height can illuminate treads to a basement kitchen. Consider noise levels. Bare wood or zinc-clad stairs look great, but the clattering of noisy kids will upset the neighbours.

Corridors also take a battering, from toddlers on trikes to the indoor roller-blading and football of older kids. Keeping corridors clutter-free makes life safer, and it's more fun for children – why shouldn't they skateboard indoors? Traditionally, ground-floor corridors double as a space to hang coats, but if the corridor is narrow, hunt elsewhere for a cloakroom. Basement entrances make a good spot, as does the back door area. Fit pegs and a storage unit, so each child has a place to stow his kit. Cylindrical containers can house cricket bats or tennis racquets, while rubber or galvanized troughs can hold outdoor shoes.

Decoratively speaking, easy-care practical surfaces are the key to good-looking traffic areas. However strict you are with the kids, small children always go upstairs with jammy hands trailing the wall, and boys inevitably kick a football about before

LEFT AND BELOW: Traffic areas need good lighting to transform them into cheerful, energetic zones and keep them safe. Swap gloomy single pendant fittings overhead for low-voltage lights, which provide clear illumination, but fit with a dimmer switch, so that at night corridors and landings are still gently lit for late-arriving teenagers or sleep-walking children.

escaping to the park. So given that halls and stairs are expensive to redecorate, choose wisely. Many interior designers swear by using abstract patterned wallpaper, as it won't show the inevitable scuffs. Painted MDF panelling or tongue and groove always looks smart. If painting in plain shades, choose muddy or deep tones in a vinyl silk or eggshell, which has a wipe-clean finish.

Flooring also takes a severe battering. While 100% wool carpet cleans up well (choose a heavy traffic variety), sisal or coir are hard-wearing, and often come in striped or heavily textured versions that don't show the dirt. If you can, fit a stair runner that starts above the level of the hall floor so that mud from careless feet won't be a problem. Limestone, ceramic tiles, parquet or floorboards are all easily washed and can be successfully combined with underfloor heating.

Traffic areas deserve dramatic decorative attention. There's no point designing light-filled imaginative rooms if the linking corridors are dark and boring. Paint corridor walls in bright shades, or choose bold flooring, such as poured rubber in a strong colour. Traffic areas are the ideal spot to display family ephemera that you, the kids and guests will all enjoy looking at. Buy cheap wooden frames, paint them all the same colour, then frame sports certificates, holiday snaps or great kids' artwork.

LEFT AND ABOVE: Try not to leave the hall and corridor walls plain and boring. If the rest of the house is decorated in all-white or neutral hues, ask the kids to pick several bright colours, and get them to help paint expanses of wall in their favourite energizing shades. Expanses of wall can be revitalized with mirrors, to reflect light into dark corners, large-scale artist's canvases, decked out in freehand stripes or dots, or a family tree, hand-painted directly onto the wall.

stockists and suppliers

FABRICS

Cath Kidston
8 Clarendon Cross
London W11 4AP
020 7221 4000
www.cathkidston.co.uk
Charming retro, floral, and spotty
fabrics and printed towelling.

Denim in Style
01666 890230
Mail order denim upholstery fabrics
in fashionable colours.

Ian Mankin
109 Regents Park Road
London NW1 8UR
020 7722 0997
Linens and washable cottons in
plains, checks and stripes.

John Lewis
Oxford Street
London W1A 1EX
020 7629 7711
www.johnlewis.com
Huge selection of furnishing fabrics,
including kids' cottons and pvc.

The Natural Fabric Company
Wessex Place
127 High Street
Hungerford
Berkshire RG17 0DL
01488 684002
Denims, calico, linens, in plains,
checks and stripes.

HARD SURFACES

Corian
0800 962116
www.corian.co.uk.
Hard-wearing surface material for
kitchens and bathrooms.

First Floor
174 Wandsworth Bridge Road
London SW6 2UQ
020 7736 1123
www.firstfloor.uk.com
Dalsouple's rubber flooring, plus
lino and vinyl. Bespoke designs.

Ray Munn
861–863 Fulham Road
London SW6 5HP
020 7736 9876
www.raymunn.com
Glitter, metallic, blackboard and
magnetic paints.

World's End Tiles
Silverthorne Road
London SW8 3HE
020 7819 2100
www.worldsendtiles.co.uk
Mosaic and ceramic wall tiles, plus
marble, slate and terracotta flooring.

FURNITURE

The Conran Shop
Michelin House
81 Fulham Road
London SW3 6RD
020 7589 7401
www.conran.com
Contemporary furniture, kids'
furniture and trendy lighting.

Habitat
0845 6010740
www.habitat.net
Modular sofas, freestanding
storage, folding and stacking
designs and funky accessories.

Ikea
020 8208 5600
www.ikea.co.uk
Storage, kids' platform and bunk
beds and sofabeds, plus budget TV,
computer and coffee tables.

Purves & Purves
220–224 Tottenham Court Road
London W1T 9QE
020 7580 8223
www.purves.co.uk
Modern indoor and outdoor
furniture and lighting, plus a kids'
range including platform beds.

FURNISHINGS/ACCESSORIES

Designers Guild
267–271 & 275–277 Kings Road
London SW3 5EN
020 7243 7300
www.designersguild.com
Bright, abstract fabrics and
wallpapers, including kids' range,
plus furniture, bedding, cushions
and tableware.

Eclectics
01843 852888
www.eclectics.co.uk
Roller, roman and Venetian blinds in
contemporary fabrics and colours,
plus sliding fabric panels.

Mathmos
22–24 Old Street
London EC1V 9AP
020 7549 2700
www.mathmos.com
Innovative, trendy lighting including
the famous lava lamp.

Marks & Spencer
0845 603 1603
www.marksandspencer.com
Freestanding storage, cosy throws,
machine washable satin bedcovers,
funky towels and kids' bedding.

Next Home
0845 600 7000
www.next.co.uk
Well-priced, fun kids' furniture and
bedding, plus storage, throws and
beanbags in fashion colours.

Photo Furnishings
Studio 019
Westbourne Studios
242 Acklam Road
London W10 5JJ
020 7575 3030
www.photo-furnishings.com
Bespoke digital printing service that
transfers any image directly onto
wallpaper, cushions or tiles.

The Rug Company
124 Holland Park Avenue
London W11 4UE
020 7229 5148
www.therugcompany.info
Quality wool rugs in modern,
animal print or traditional designs.

KIDS FURNITURE/ACCESSORIES

Bump
020 7249 7000
www.bumpstuff.com
Excellent ready-to-paint MDF kids'
beds, including sleigh and bunk
bed styles.

Junior Living
293 Fulham Road
London SW10 9PZ
020 7376 5001
www.juniorliving.co.uk
Modern and traditional kids'
furniture ranges, from beds to desks.

lionwitchwardrobe
020 8265 8449
www.lionwitchwardrobe.co.uk
Beautifully designed contemporary
oak furniture for children.

Oreka Kids
020 8804 2045
www.orekakids.com
Range of scaled down childrens'
furniture, from a wardrobe to a
storage bench, in birch plywood.

Wigwam Kids
0870 902 7500
www.wigwamkids.co.uk
Mail order furniture for babies, girls
and boys.

STORAGE

The Holding Company
241-245 Kings Road
London SW3 5EL
020 7352 1600
www.theholdingcompany.co.uk
Large choice of storage boxes, from
acrylic to rattan baskets, as well as
freestanding storage and wardrobe
storage systems.

Lakeland
015394 88100
www.lakelandlimited.co.uk
Mail order catalogue with big
selection of useful storage boxes,
hooks and clothes hanging rails.

Muji
16–17 Tottenham Court Road
London W1P 9DP
(020) 7323 2208
www.muji.co.uk
Storage boxes and units, foldaway
furniture and clothes rails.

PARENTS' ROOMS

Earth Tones Collection
020 8965 9994
www.earthtones.co.uk
Leather beanbags, fairy lights and
throws.

Melin Tregwynt
Castlemorris
Haverfordwest
Pembrokeshire SA62 5UX
01348 891225
www.melintregwynt.co.uk
Wool rugs, throws and cushions in
stripes, abstracts and checks.

Monsoon Home
336 Kings Road
London SW3 4LY
020 7313 3000
www.monsoon.co.uk
Beautiful fashion throws, cushions
and sparkly accessories.

Musa
31 Holland Street
London W8 4NA
020 7937 6282
Source of antique chandeliers,
Venetian mirrors and contemporary
designer labels.

Plumo
0870 241 3590
www.plumo.com
Mail-order catalogue featuring
Eastern-inspired low seating,
pouffes, floor cushions and throws.

MEDIA ROOMS

Gibson Music
Unit 8, The Broomhouse
50 Sulivan Road
London SW6 3DX
020 7384 2270
www.gibson-music.com
Specialists in home entertainment
music and computer systems.

MAIL-ORDER CATALOGUES

Akta
020 7625 7770
www.akta.co.uk
Funky kids' seating, lighting and
accessories.

The Great Little Trading Company
0870 850 6000
www.gltc.co.uk
Specialist kids' catalogue including
mini furniture, storage solutions,
beanbags and safety gadgets.

McCord
0870 908 7005
www.emccord.com
Freestanding storage, decorative
hooks, rugs, beanbags, kids'
furniture and kitchen stools.

Oka
0870 1606002
www.okadirect.com
Rattan, lacquer and leather storage
boxes, sophisticated seating cubes
and floor cushions.

Pedlars
01330 850400,
www.pedlars.co.uk
Everything from go-carts to fleece
blankets in stripes and camouflage
and a great outdoor teepee.

Urchin
0870 720 0709
www.urchin.co.uk
Play tables, desks, mini kids'
furniture, pinboards and lighting.

The White Company
0870 900 9555
www.thewhiteco.com
Towels and bedding for grown-ups
and children, luxurious throws and
colourful kids' bean cubes.

OUTDOOR FURNITURE AND ACCESSORIES

Big Game Hunters
08701 501511
www.gardengames.co.uk
Everything from croquet and giant
chess to trampolines and space
hoppers.

The Modern Gardening Company
01279 851900
www.moderngarden.co.uk
Colourful modern garden furniture.

Timberline
01246 260099
www.timberline.co.uk
Hardwood climbing frames,
playhouses and accessories from
sandpits to tyre swings.

Social Climbers
01235 751717
www.socialclimbers.co.uk
Cape Cod style playhouses,
climbing walls and play frames.

picture credits

All photography by Debi Treloar (unless stated otherwise)
Key: a=above, b=below, r=right, l=left, c=centre.

1 Imogen Chappel's home in Suffolk; 2 Paul Balland and Jane Wadham of jwflowers.com's family home in London; 3 A family home in Manhattan, designed by architect Amanda Martocchio and Gustavo Martinez Design; 4 Kristiina Ratia and Jeff Gocke's family home in Norwalk, Connecticut; 5 New-build house in Notting Hill designed by Seth Stein Architects; 8 al Architect Simon Colebrook's home in London; 8 ac & br House by Knott Architects in London; 8 ar & bc Family home, Bankside, London; 8 cl Sarah Munro and Brian Ayling's home in London; 8 c Ian Hogarth's family home; 8 cr & bl A family home in London; photographs by Erwin Wurm; 9 House by Knott Architects in London; 10 a A Fifth Avenue Residence, New York City designed by Bruce Bierman Design, Inc.; 10 b Paul Balland and Jane Wadham of jwflowers.com's family home in London; 11 Imogen Chappel's home in Suffolk; 12–13 Kristiina Ratia and Jeff Gocke's family home in Norwalk, Connecticut; 14-15 Architect Simon Colebrook's home in London; 16-17 Kate and Dominic Ash's home in London; 18-19 New-build house in Notting Hill designed by Seth Stein Architects; 20 A family home in West London; 21 Catherine Chermayeff & Jonathan David's family home in New York, designed by Asfour Guzy Architects; 22-23 A family home in Manhattan, designed by architect Amanda Martocchio and Gustavo Martinez Design; 24-25 Imogen Chappel's home in Suffolk; 26 a Family home, Bankside, London; 26 b Ian Hogarth's family home; 27 A Fifth Avenue Residence, New York City designed by Bruce Bierman Design, Inc.; 28 Robert Elms and Christina Wilson's family home in London; 29 The Swedish Chair – Lena Renkel Eriksson; 30 a A family home in West London; 30 b Catherine Chermayeff & Jonathan David's family home in New York, designed by Asfour Guzy Architects; 31 The Swedish Chair – Lena Renkel Eriksson; 32 A family home in West London; 33 A family home in London; photographs by Erwin Wurm; 34-37 al Catherine Chermayeff & Jonathan David's family home in New York, designed by Asfour Guzy Architects; 37 c Robert Elms and Christina Wilson's family home in London; 37 b Paul Balland and Jane Wadham of jwflowers.com's family home in London; 37 ar Sarah Munro and Brian Ayling's home in London; 38-39 A family home in London; portraits by artist Julian Opie, Lisson Gallery; 40-41 Sarah Munro and Brian Ayling's home in London; paintings by Brian Ayling; 42-43 A family home in Manhattan, designed by architect Amanda Martocchio and Gustavo Martinez Design; 44-45 Jill Henry & Jon Pellicoro's family home in New York. Artwork by Jon Pellicoro; 46 A family home in Manhattan, designed by architect Amanda Martocchio and Gustavo Martinez Design; 47 Catherine Chermayeff & Jonathan David's family home in New York, designed by Asfour Guzy Architects; 48-49 House by Knott Architects in London; 50-51 A family home in London; 52 al Imogen Chappel's home in Suffolk; 52 acl A family home in Manhattan, designed by architect Amanda Martocchio and Gustavo Martinez Design; 52 bl A family home in West London; 52 ar Catherine Chermayeff & Jonathan David's family home in New York, designed by Asfour Guzy Architects; 52 cl Robert Elms and Christina Wilson's family home in London; 52 br The Swedish Chair – Lena Renkel Eriksson; 53 al Robert Elms and Christina Wilson's family home in London; 53 acl Kate and Dominic Ash's home in London; 53 acr A Fifth Avenue Residence, New York City designed by Bruce Bierman Design, Inc.; 53 ar Imogen Chappel's home in Suffolk; 53 b Paul Balland and Jane Wadham of jwflowers.com's family home in London; 54 Robert Elms and Christina Wilson's family home in London; 55 a Jill Henry & Jon Pellicoro's family home in New York. Artwork by Jon Pellicoro; 55 br Ian Hogarth's family home; 55 bl Catherine Chermayeff & Jonathan David's family home in New York, designed by Asfour Guzy Architects; 56-57 Kate and Dominic Ash's home in London; 58 l Kristiina Ratia and Jeff Gocke's family home in Norwalk, Connecticut; 58 ar A family home in West London; 58 br Sarah Munro and Brian Ayling's home in London; 59 a A family home in London; 59 b Architect Simon Colebrook's home in London; 60 al New-build house in Notting Hill designed by Seth Stein Architects; 60 ac Fifth Avenue Residence, New York City designed by Bruce Bierman Design, Inc.; 60 ar Ian Hogarth's family home; 60 cl Imogen Chappel's home in Suffolk; 60 c & bc A family home in West London; 60 cr Sarah Munro and Brian Ayling's home in London; paintings by Brian Ayling; 60 bl & br Robert Elms and Christina Wilson's family home in London; 61 A family home in West London; 62 a Catherine Chermayeff & Jonathan David's family home in New York, designed by Asfour Guzy Architects; 62 b Kate and Dominic Ash's home in London; 63 Ian Hogarth's family home; 64 & 65 b House by Knott Architects in London; 65 a Kate and Dominic Ash's home in London; 66 A family home in Manhattan, designed by architect Amanda Martocchio and Gustavo Martinez Design; 67 Family home, Bankside, London; 68 Paul Balland and Jane Wadham of jwflowers.com's family home in London; 69 Catherine Chermayeff &

Jonathan David's family home in New York, designed by Asfour Guzy Architects; 70-71 New-build house in Notting Hill designed by Seth Stein Architects; 72-73 A family home in West London; 74 al Imogen Chapel's home in Suffolk; 74 acl & b Ian Hogarth's family home; 74 ar House by Knott Architects in London; 75 al & ar Kristiina Ratia and Jeff Gocke's family home in Norwalk, Connecticut; 75 acl & cr New-build house in Notting Hill designed by Seth Stein Architects; 75 acr & bl Imogen Chapel's home in Suffolk; 75 br Kate and Dominic Ash's home in London; 76 al Kristiina Ratia and Jeff Gocke's family home in Norwalk, Connecticut; 76 ar Imogen Chapel's home in Suffolk; 76 b Sarah Munro and Brian Ayling's home in London; paintings by Brian Ayling; 77 Kristiina Ratia and Jeff Gocke's family home in Norwalk, Connecticut; 78 b Robert Elms and Christina Wilson's family home in London; 79 A family home in London; 80-81 Catherine Chermayeff & Jonathan David's family home in New York, designed by Asfour Guzy Architects; 82-83 Paul Balland and Jane Wadham of jwflowers.com's family home in London; 84-85 Kristiina Ratia and Jeff Gocke's family home in Norwalk, Connecticut; 86 al A family home in Manhattan, designed by architect Amanda Martocchio and Gustavo Martinez Design; 86 ac & ar A family home in West London; 86 cl The Swedish Chair – Lena Renkel Eriksson; 86 bl A Fifth Avenue Residence, New York City designed by Bruce Bierman Design, Inc.; 86 br Kate and Dominic Ash's home in London; 87 l A family home in Manhattan, designed by architect Amanda Martocchio and Gustavo Martinez Design; 87 c A Fifth Avenue Residence, New York City designed by Bruce Bierman Design, Inc.; 87 r Robert Elms and Christina Wilson's family home in London; 88-89 House by Knott Architects in London; 90 Family home, Bankside, London; 91 Ian Hogarth's family home; 92-93 New-build house in Notting Hill designed by Seth Stein Architects; 94 a Imogen Chappel's home in Suffolk; 94 b A family home in West London; 95 Robert Elms and Christina Wilson's family home in London; 96-97 Architect Simon Colebrook's home in London; 98-99 New-build house in Notting Hill designed by Seth Stein Architects; 100-101 Kristiina Ratia and Jeff Gocke's family home in Norwalk, Connecticut; 102 Sarah Munro and Brian Ayling's home in London; paintings by Brian Ayling; 103 Ian Hogarth's family home; 104 al Imogen Chappel's home in Suffolk; 104 ar & b The Swedish Chair – Lena Renkel Eriksson; 105 Catherine Chermayeff & Jonathan David's family home in New York, designed by Asfour Guzy Architects; 106 al & br A family home in West London; 106 ac, cl & c Kristiina Ratia and Jeff Gocke's family home in Norwalk, Connecticut; 106 ar Architect Simon Colebrook's home in London; 106 bl New-build house in Notting Hill designed by Seth Stein Architects; 106 bc & 107 House by Knott Architects in London; 108 a Architect Simon Colebrook's home in London; 108 b A family home in West London; 110-111 Kristiina Ratia and Jeff Gocke's family home in Norwalk, Connecticut; 112-113 New-build house in Notting Hill designed by Seth Stein Architects; 114 br House by Knott Architects in London; 115 a Sarah Munro and Brian Ayling's home in London; 115 b Family home, Bankside, London; 116 Architect Simon Colebrook's home in London; 117 House by Knott Architects in London; 118-119 Catherine Chermayeff & Jonathan David's family home in New York, designed by Asfour Guzy Architects; 120 a Ian Hogarth's family home; 120 b & 121 Catherine Chermayeff & Jonathan David's family home in New York, designed by Asfour Guzy Architects; 122 & 123 br Kate and Dominic Ash's home in London; 123 a New-build house in Notting Hill designed by Seth Stein Architects; 123 bl Architect Simon Colebrook's home in London; 124 & 125 ar Family home, Bankside, London; 125 al New-build house in Notting Hill designed by Seth Stein Architects; 125 b Ian Hogarth's family home; 126 al The Swedish Chair – Lena Renkel Eriksson; 126 ar Sarah Munro and Brian Ayling's home in London; 126 b & 127 l Family home, Bankside, London; 127 r A family home in Manhattan, designed by architect Amanda Martocchio and Gustavo Martinez Design; 128 al Catherine Chermayeff & Jonathan David's family home in New York, designed by Asfour Guzy Architects; 128 ac Kate and Dominic Ash's home in London; 128 ar, c & br The Swedish Chair – Lena Renkel Eriksson; 128 bl Family home, Bankside, London; 129 al & acl Kate and Dominic Ash's home in London; 129 ar Catherine Chermayeff & Jonathan David's family home in New York, designed by Asfour Guzy Architects; 129 c Imogen Chappel's home in Suffolk; 129 b Robert Elms and Christina Wilson's family home in London; 130 b A family home in West London; 131 Sarah Munro and Brian Ayling's home in London; 132 a Paul Balland and Jane Wadham of jwflowers.com's family home in London; 132 b Architect Simon Colebrook's home in London; 133 House by Knott Architects in London; 134 al A family home in Manhattan, designed by architect Amanda Martocchio and Gustavo Martinez Design; 134 ar & br House by Knott Architects in London; 134 bl The Swedish Chair – Lena Renkel Eriksson; 135 l Jill Henry & Jon Pellicoro's family home in New York; 135 r Kristiina Ratia and Jeff Gocke's family home in Norwalk, Connecticut; 136 l & br Ian Hogarth's family home; 136 ar & 137 b Family home, Bankside, London; 137 a A Fifth Avenue Residence, New York City designed by Bruce Bierman Design, Inc.; 144 House by Knott Architects in London.

architects and designers whose work is featured in this book:

Asfour Guzy Architects
594 Broadway
New York, NY 10012
t. + 1 212 334 9350
email: easfour@asfourguzy.com
Pages 21, 30 b, 34–37 al, 47, 52 ar,
55 br, 62 a, 69, 80–81, 105, 118–
119, 120 b, 121, 128 al, 129 ar

Also involved in this project:
Cutting Edge Construction
71 Hudson Ave
Brooklyn, NY 11201
t/f. + 1 718 965 3027

Dominic Ash
Unit 7 Links Yard
29 Spelman Street
London E1 5LQ
t. 020 7377 1982
email: dominic@dominicash.co.uk
www.dominicash.co.uk
Pages 16–17, 53 acl, 56–57, 62 b,
65 a, 75 br, 86 br, 122, 123 br,
128 ac, 129 al & acr

Brian Ayling, Artist
t. 020 8802 9853
Pages 8 cl, 37 ar, 40–41, 58 br,
60 cr, 76 b, 102, 115 a, 126 ar, 131

Bruce Bierman Design, Inc.
29 West 15 Street
New York, NY 10011
t.001 212.243.1935
f.001 212.243.6615
www.biermandesign.com
Pages 10 a, 27, 53 acr, 60 ac,
86 bl, 87 c, 137 a

Imogen Chappel
07803 156 081
Pages 1, 11, 24-25, 52 al, 53 ar, 60
cl, 74 al, 75 acr & bl, 76 ar, 94 a,
104 al, 129 c

Simon Colebrook, Architect
Douglas Stephen Partnership
140–142 St John Street

London EC1V 4UB
t. 020 7336 7884
f. 020 7336 7841
email: dsp@dspl.co.uk
www.dspl.co.uk

Also involved in this project:
Packman WCAS Engineers
BDA Quantity Surveyors
Pages 8 al, 14–15, 59 b, 96–97,
106 ar, 108 a, 116, 123 bl, 132 b

Dive Architects
10 Park Street
London SE1 9AB
t. 020 7407 0955
email: mail@divearchitects.com
www.divearchitects.com
Pages 8 ar & bc, 26 a, 67, 90, 115
b, 124, 125 ar, 126 b, 127 l, 128 bl,
136 ar, 137 b

Gustavo Martinez Design
206 Fifth Avenue
4th Floor
New York NY 10010
t.+ 1 212 686 3102
f.+ 1 212 686 3104
email: gmdecor@aol.com
Pages 3, 22–23, 42–43, 46, 52 acl,
66, 86 al, 87 l, 127 r, 134 al

jwflowers.com
Unit E8 & 9
1–45 Durham Street
London SE11 5JH
t. 020 7735 7771
f. 020 7735 2011
email: jane@jwflowers.com
www.jwflowers.com
Pages 2, 10 b, 37 b, 53 b, 82–83,
132 a

Knott Architects
98b Tollington Park
London N4 3RB
t. 020 7263 8844
f. 020 7263 4700
email: mail@knottarchitects.co.uk

www.knottarchitects.co.uk
Pages 8 ac & br, 9, 48–49, 64, 65
b, 74 ar, 88–89, 106 bc, 107, 114
br, 117, 134 ar & br

Kristiina Ratia Designs
t. + 1 203 852 0027
Pages 4, 12–13, 58 l, 75 al & ar,
76 al, 77, 84–85, 100–101, 106 ac,
cl & c, 110–111, 135 r

Littman Goddard Hogarth
12 Chelsea Wharf
15 Lots Road
London SW10 9AS
t. 020 7351 7871
f. 020 7351 4110
email: info@lgh-architects.co.uk
www.lgh-architects.co.uk
Pages 8 c, 26 b, 55 bl, 60 ar, 63,
74 acl & b, 91, 103, 120a, 125 b,
136 l & br

Amanda Martocchio, Architect
189 Brushy Ridge Road
New Canaan, CT 06840
Pages 3, 22–23, 42–43, 46, 52 acl,
66, 86 al, 87 l, 127 r, 134 al

Musa
31 Holland Street
London W8 4NA
t. 020 7937 6282
A source of antique chandeliers
and Venetian mirrors plus
contemporary designer labels and
vintage clothing
Pages 20, 30 a, 32, 52 bl, 58 ar, 60 c
& bc, 61, 72–73, 74 acr, 86 ac & ar,
94 b, 106 al & br, 108 b, 130 b

Jon Pellicoro, Artist
email: mhfny@inch.com
Pages 44–45, 55 a, 68, 135 l

Nico Rensch
Architeam
www.architeam.co.uk

Pages 8 cr & bl, 33, 38-39, 50-51,
59 a, 79

Seth Stein Architects
15 Grand Union Centre
West Row
Ladbroke Grove
London W10 5AS
t. 020 8968 8581
f. 020 8968 8591
www.sethstein.com
Pages 5, 18–19, 60 al, 70–71, 75
acl & cr, 92–93, 98–99, 106 bl,
112–113, 123 a, 125 al, 133

The Swedish Chair
t. 020 8657 8560
email: lena@theswedishchair.com
www.theswedishchair.com
Pages 29, 31, 52 br, 86 cl, 104 ar &
b, 126 al, 128 ar, c & br, 134 bl,
endpaper

Also involved in this project:
David Sandstrom, Painter
Decorative paintings and murals
t. +46 90 98049

Cecilie Telle, Knitted Felt Designer
email: cecilietelle@hotmail.com
www.amimono.demon.co.uk
Pages 8 ac & br, 9, 48–49, 64, 65
b, 74 ar, 88–89, 106 bc, 107, 114
br, 117, 134 ar & br

Christina Wilson, Interiors Stylist
email: christinawilson@btopenworld.com
Pages 28, 37 c, 52 cl, 53 al, 54, 60
bl & br, 78 b, 87 r, 95, 129 b

Thanks also to:
Heiberg Cummings Design
548 West 28th Street # 510
New York, NY 10001
t.001 212 239 4470
f.001 212 239 4830
email: WCummings@hcd3.com
www.hcd3.com

index

Page numbers in *italic* refer to captions and illustrations

acknowledgments

Thank you, Alison Starling and David Peters of Ryland Peters and Small, for asking me to write a book devoted to family living, a subject close to my heart! Thanks to Annabel Morgan, for being an impeccable editor, and to Fiona Lindsay of Limelight Management, for her enthusiastic support. Thanks also to Gabriella Le Grazie and Fiona Walker, for vibrant art direction, and to Claire Hector for so efficiently sourcing great locations.

Thank you, Debi Treloar, for such fresh and beautiful photographs, which perfectly capture the essence of kids at home. And to all the families who invited us into their busy but beautiful private spaces, so the rest of us can be inspired!

Thanks to my parents Harry and Ann, and my sister, Sally, for making my first taste of family life such fun. But especially, thanks to Anthony, Cicely and Felix, because we've had the best time creating our own family home, be it tidy, messy or somewhere in between.